An Ey [illegible] Look at Edmonton's History

Shane Blakely

© First Edition
November 2024

Introduction

Since childhood I always enjoyed flying. I often went with my father Murray, an airborne traffic reporter, over the City of Edmonton. As a five-year-old, I found it a thrill to get up in the air and see the world from a different perspective. I was so comfortable in a four-seat airplane that I often fell asleep. When I found an interest in photography, I would always take my camera with me on the flights so I could share the views I had with my friends. It paid off one flight when a warehouse fire started. Realizing the images I captured, I approached The Edmonton Journal to show the editor what I photographed. He liked them and printed one, giving me my first published photo when I was in my mid-teens. I found myself in the same situation again, photographing the devastating destruction after a series of tornados passed through the city.

I would routinely photograph places across the city that interested me, West Edmonton Mall, Commonwealth Stadium and events that were happening. When my father retired, I didn't get to fly whenever I wanted, I started to miss it. I had to get my pilot's licence to get my feet off the ground once again. Shortly after receiving my licence, I was hired to fly in the Global One News Helicopter to do what my father did and fly over the city to report on traffic. When the pandemic happened, it was tough doing traffic reports when most people stayed home, there was few vehicles on the streets. Most stores were closed, no events or public gatherings were happening. Needing to find something to talk about from the chopper, I started a history segment, bringing historical buildings to the forefront. To my surprise, many viewers enjoyed them and asked if I had them in a book. I always answered no, so I thought, why not. Here they are!

Contents - All stories are listed alphabetically

A. MacDonald Building

105 Avenue and 102 Street

The A. MacDonald Building, constructed in 1913, holds a significant place in Edmonton's history. Its proximity to the former Canadian National Railway yards in downtown made it a crucial part of the city's development. Named after Alexander MacDonald, President of the A. MacDonald Company of Winnipeg, the Edmonton warehouse became one of northern Alberta's three largest grocery suppliers. MacDonald's Consolidated was a pioneer wholesale grocery distributor in Western Canada and became one of the largest suppliers in Northern Alberta.

This was their distribution centre for the developing areas to the north and west of the city, as most of the supplies were shipped by rail. They occupied this warehouse from 1914 to 1949. As roads were constructed and trucks became the more convenient way to transport their products, MacDonald's Consolidated built a new warehouse in 1965 that still operates today at the Yellowhead Trail and 142 Street.

Acacia Masonic Hall

83 Avenue and 104 Street

The Masons date back to 1897 in this area. They moved a few times in Old Strathcona, including the Richards Block behind this structure, before they purchased this piece of land in 1914. Construction started 15 years later, in June 1929.

It opened in October of the same year at a cost of $30,000. Alberta's first premier, Alexander Rutherford, was the first Worshipful Master in this building. They still have the first 'minutes book' with his signature.

Over the years, the building has been upgraded, including in 2002, but the major one happened in 1981 when an extension was added to the back to incorporate a kitchen and storage space.

This place is still going strong 95 years later. It is open for rentals, such as for weddings and concerts, and is used by the Fringe Festival.

Air Traffic Control Tower

at ***City Centre Airport***

Initially called Blatchford Field, this was the first licenced airfield in Canada when it opened in 1927. Over its 86-year history, the airport has had many names, including Edmonton Municipal Airport, Edmonton Industrial Airport, Edmonton City Centre Airport, and Blatchford Field at Edmonton City Centre Airport. The control tower was built between September 1971 and April 1972 for $300,000 and officially opened on May 1, 1972, at 7:30 AM.

Air traffic across Northern Alberta was controlled from City Centre Airport before the International Airport opened on November 15, 1960. The federal government privatized air services in 1996, which created Nav Canada to manage air traffic nationwide. They have 4000+ employees who operate 96 air traffic facilities. There are just under 1600 registered sites, including 370 heliports. They worked at this tower until it was de-commissioned on November 30, 2013. Today, the tower remains a reminder of the airport's history, which was here for over eight decades.

Alberta Aviation Museum

Kingsway and 116 Street

Built at Blatchford Field in 1941, it was designated Hangar 14. The hangar was one of the facilities being built across the country for the British Commonwealth Air Training Plan, its purpose was to train aircrews in Canada for duty in the Second World War.

Edmonton was the location for the Initial Training, a Flying School, and an Air Observers School. Hangars built for the Air Training Plan were of a standard design that could be doubled in width and depth. Hangar 14 is a doublewide and double-long model and is the only remaining hangar of that type still standing in Canada.

When the war ended, Hangar 14 became the home of the Royal Canadian Air Force 418 City of Edmonton Squadron. It remained so until 1956 when they moved to the new air base at Namao, north of the city. From 1957 to 1991, the building served a variety of purposes. Since 1991, it has been the home of the Edmonton Aviation Heritage Society, and it was designated as a provincial historic resource in 2000. Today, they have the third-largest collection of aircraft on display in Canada.

Alberta Hospital

Fort Road and 174 Avenue

The Department of Education planned building number one for children, but it was soon taken over by the Health Department as the Provincial Mental Institute when it opened on July 1, 1923. Initially, 47 patients were being treated for 'shell shock' from World War I.

Over the decades, this hospital facility has grown to 45 structures. The buildings were named numerically in the order in which they were built. The hospital was completely self-sufficient from the beginning. They have a water tower, a sewage disposal plant, a greenhouse, a garden, a power plant that still heats and lights the campus, and a fire department. Those firefighters were the first to respond to the nearby Evergreen Trailer Park when the tornado hit in 1987. By the 1950s, there were almost 3,000 patient beds. In the 1980s, there were 650 beds, and today, there are 340.

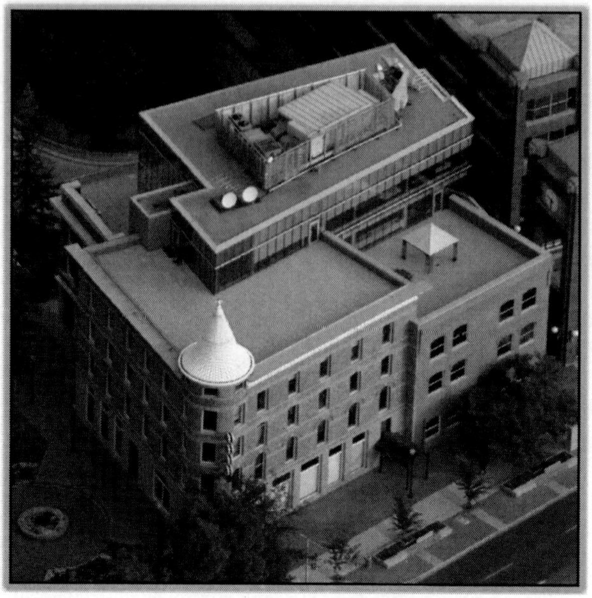

Alberta Hotel

Jasper Avenue and 97 Street

When the Alberta Hotel was built in 1903, it was highly regarded as one of the finest hotels west of Winnipeg and the most fashionable establishment in Edmonton. It included the finest bar and restaurant in the district. Here, is where Prime Minister Wilfred Laurier stayed when he proclaimed Alberta a province in 1905.

The Alberta Hotel, a pioneer in many aspects, can boast several 'firsts' in Edmonton and Alberta. It was the first to introduce a passenger elevator, the first four-storey building, and the first major brick structure on Jasper Avenue. It also led the way in hotel amenities, being the first in Edmonton to offer shower baths, telephones, and a call-bell system for guest convenience.

The Alberta Hotel was carefully dismantled in 1984 to make way for Canada Place, and then it was moved 50 feet west. The exterior was reconstructed with a modern interior, and now it is the home of CKUA radio, which has been broadcasting in Edmonton since 1927.

Alex Taylor School

Jasper Avenue and 93 Street

This structure opened in 1908, during Edmonton's most significant economic boom. The school was named to honour Alexander Taylor, a pioneer, telegraph operator and Edmonton Public School Board chairman. It has survived several fires, a landslide, and even a threat to bulldoze it for a road.

In 1914, the school launched a program to provide lunches for the children. If they could pay, the cost was two cents for a cup of milk and one cent for each slice of buttered bread.

The school, a cornerstone of the community, served for 93 years before closing its doors in 2001.

Anglican Parish of Christ Church

121 Street and 102 Avenue

The original Christ Church was built in 1909. It was a small building not far from this location, but as the congregation grew, the building became over crowded. It was relocated to 102 Avenue, the former site of the Glenora Tennis and Skating Club. With some remodelling, it became a temporary location until members could raise more money for a permanent church.

When all the money had been raised, construction commenced in 1920, and they decided to stay here. As the church community grew, a parish hall and a bell tower were added.

Annamoe Mansion

100 Avenue and 120 Street

Annamoe means cattle crossing in Irish. That is where this place received its name, after the town in Ireland. Robert Barton lived there. He financed this place for his cousin, who lived here.

It was called a mansion but is an apartment building with twenty-five units. This was one of several apartments built before the First World War along 100th Avenue, along with the Westminster Apartments and the LeMarchand Mansion.

Annamoe was built for the white-collared worker and had many modern features, including electric doorbells, a freight elevator powered by hand-pulled rope, and a dumb waiter in each unit to send trash to the basement. Over one hundred years later, Annamoe is still an active apartment building with no historic designation.

Apache Seeds Building

149 Street and Stony Plain Road

The first location of this store opened around the corner in 1958 when it was a part of the Town of Jasper Place. They quickly outgrew the small store and moved into a larger space in 1964. They offered various services, including window repair and skate sharpening, and were one of the first in the city to sell skidoos. It was the gardening supplies that brought customers in. They grew again when they expanded to the building beside it. The business is still family-run, and they are still sticking to their values of selling seeds, soil, and fertilizer, and in the winter months, they sell shovels and ice melt. This place was featured in a national gardening publication.

With the LRT construction around the corner, it is hurting some businesses and helping others, such as this one. As the long line of motorists wait for the traffic light to change, many notice this place and pull into their parking lot. The same sign from the 1960s still welcomes everyone. Apache Seeds celebrated its 65th anniversary in 2023.

Archibald Block

82 Avenue and 105 Street

Seymour Archibald moved to this area from Nova Scotia in 1898. He had just graduated as a doctor, and at the time, there were only nine other doctors in the Greater Edmonton Area. Canadian Pacific Railway hired him a year later to serve as their District Medical Officer.

Like many others at the time, he became a real estate mogul and scooped up the odd lot or two where he could. One of his holdings caught the interest of the Government. In 1909, he parted with one of his properties for $10,000, and it would become the Southside Post Office. With that money, Archibald got to work on his own building, as construction began that same year at a cost of $13,000.

For the first couple of decades, this place housed a drug store, a clothing store, a jeweller, a plumbing shop, a confectionary, and a fresh fruit wholesaler.

Not only was Dr. Archibald CPR's Chief Medical Officer, but he was also a World War I veteran, a founding member of the Mayfair Golf and Country Club, and a Masonic Lodge member.

While this may not be the most beautiful building, it is strongly connected to one of Northern Alberta's first professional doctors.

Armstrong Block

104 Street and 101 Avenue

This structure was built in 1912 in the heart of the warehouse district in Edmonton's downtown. A rail line used to run behind the building, connecting the warehouses along the street to the CN Rail mainline on 104 Avenue. Edmonton was expanding quickly, there was high demand for residential, commercial, and warehouse space. This building was designed to include all three. Wholesale businesses like the Brown Fruit Company and General Motors used the basement and first floor. The first and second floors were office space for brokerage companies, investors, and the French Consulate. The remainder of the building were apartments. It is the only remaining heritage building specifically built for mixed-use. In 2003, the Armstrong Block received its historic recognition.

Arndt Building

81 Avenue and 101 Street

The exact date of construction is not known, but the first listing of this address was in 1928 as Ted Arndt's Blacksmith Shop. Records show renovations happened here in 1938 and again in 1943. By the 1950s, this business had changed from a blacksmith to a machine shop, with the discovery of oil in Alberta and the nearby rail yard.

After more renovations, this place became a restaurant. The building received its Municipal Historic designation in 2009.

Athabasca, Assiniboia and Pembina Halls

University of Alberta Campus, 115 Street and Saskatchewan Drive

These three Gothic-style buildings are the first on the University's Campus. Athabasca Hall (in center) was completed in 1911, followed by Assiniboia Hall (right) in 1912 and Pembina Hall (left) in 1914. They are nicknamed the 'Three Sisters' since they are almost identical.

From the beginning, the buildings contained the offices of the President, lecture rooms, laboratories, and a library.

Students lived in the residence wings, which had separate areas for men, women, and married couples. Some staff also lived under the same roof. In 1915, with the opening of the Arts Building, the halls were changed to just student housing; Pembina Hall was the women's residence.

These buildings served as student residences until the construction of Lister Centre in 1962, then Assiniboia Hall was repurposed into office space. The three buildings were initially slated for demolition, but due to strong opposition, they were saved and upgraded.

In 1976, Athabasca and Assiniboia Halls received steel and concrete frames to replace the original wood ones. Pembina was used for residence until 2003, but now all three buildings serve as faculty and staff offices.

Balfour Manor

116 Street and 101 Avenue

Balfour Manor was built in 1912 as Fire Hall #4. It served the developing west end of downtown and was designed for the horse-drawn equipment that was stationed there. The fire department briefly replaced the horses with fire trucks as they were only open for nine years. 1921, the fire station was closed; it was re-purposed as a garage, an office for a mail contractor, and a bus company garage. When there was a short supply of homes during World War II, the building was again re-purposed into ten-one-bedroom apartments in 1939.

The original brick pavements for the fire hall remain under the front lawn. The original furnace still heats this place. It is the second oldest furnace in the province that is still operating, although it doesn't burn coal anymore. This place received its historic designation in 2005.

Beaver House

103 Street and 101 Avenue

Constructed in 1929, as the name says, this was a beaver house. It was used as a beaver pelt trading post for the Hudson's Bay Company. As the years passed and HBC moved into retail, this structure became their warehouse for the nearby store. After selling this place, it was used by several businesses before being restored, reclaiming the bricks and wood frame, then converting it to retail and office space in 2009.

Bennett School

94 Street and 97 Avenue

Constructed in 1912, it opened a year later, during the first economic boom. It was named after Thomas Bennett, the first mayor of Strathcona. During the great flood of 1915, many residents sought shelter on the second floor to avoid the rising waters that destroyed many homes.

Bennett School is one of three schools built in the river valley, but this is the only one south of the river. It served the community for 60 years before it was closed in 1973. This place received a second lease on life when it became office space for the 1978 Commonwealth Games and the Capital City Parks Authority. In 1981, the school board opened it again; this time, it became the Bennett Environmental Education Centre. This place is now for day and overnight school programs, environmental lessons, and outdoor activities. This structure is on the city's list, waiting for its historic designation.

Beverly Cenotaph Park

118 Avenue and 40 Street

The Town of Beverly was home to just under 1,000 people during the First World War. One hundred seventy men served in the war effort, and twenty-seven died in action.

Thomas Dando, a veteran, Beverly's postmaster, and mayor donated two lots of land, to preserve their memory. Other residents and businesses donated money and materials to construct this marble and concrete cenotaph, which took only six months to complete.

Initially called Memorial Park to remember the fallen soldiers, this Cenotaph was unveiled on October 17, 1920. Dignitaries at the ceremony included Lieutenant Governor George Brett, Brigadier-General William Griesbach, Edmonton Mayor Joe Clarke, and Beverly Mayor Fred Humberstone.

The Cenotaph is the oldest war memorial in Alberta.

Re-dedication ceremonies have taken place a couple of times. Once in 1958, when more than 1,000 people turned out, and again in 2017. This monument was declared a Municipal Historic Resource in 2016.

Beverly Train Bridge

Located at the east end of the Yellowhead Trail

Originally called the Grand Trunk Pacific Bridge, it was named after the rail company that built it. Grand Trunk Railroad was moving west from Winnipeg, and instead of going directly to the downtown area, they wanted an east entrance to the city. The train bridge stood alone here for 45 years before the vehicle bridge opened in 1953. Construction on the train bridge started in 1906. It took two years to complete, with as many as 300 men working on it at one time.

Upon its opening, the Beverly Train Bridge, a marvel of engineering, claimed the title of the largest bridge in the province. Standing at a towering height of 138 feet and stretching over a length of 1,655 feet, it was a sight to behold.

Birks Building

Jasper Avenue and 104 Street

Henry Birks and Sons began their business in Montreal in 1879. They were descendants of a family of silversmiths who had practiced their trade in England since the 15th century. In 1927, Birks bought the successful jewelry store owned by D.A. Kirkland, the "Diamond Prince of Edmonton." They constructed this building for $350,000. Over 5,000 people attended the opening of the store in November of 1929.

In keeping with company policy across Canada, Birks reserved most of the office space on the upper floors for medical and dental offices as a public service. This was the first building in Edmonton designed primarily for medical offices.

In 1934, the fourth floor was home to CJCA Radio. With their memorable Flying Tiger sign on the roof, they stayed there for 39 years before moving. The building now has street-level retail space with offices on the upper floors.

This building and the one in Montreal are the only original Birks buildings still standing in Canada.

Blue Cross Animal Hospital Building

97 Street and 111 Avenue

This was the first building in the city constructed specifically to be used as a veterinary clinic when it opened in 1948. It was set up to look after small animals such as dogs and cats. Inside were kennels, an x-ray room, and an operating room. There have only been four veterinarians who have owned the building over the 70 years of operation. When this structure was sold in 2018, the new owners applied and received a historic designation to preserve it, then changed it into a law firm, cafe, and art gallery.

Boardwalk Building

102 Avenue and 103 Street

In 1910, the Ross Brothers built this hardware store and warehouse. It was considered one of the most modern in Western Canada at the time. Two years later, the Revillon Building was constructed next to it as a distribution centre. These two buildings quickly became the centre of Edmonton's commercial and warehouse district prior to the First World War. Additions were made in 1928 and 1940, even though other companies worked from here, such as the J.W. Ashdown Hardware Company this building remained a hardware store until 1970. The building, showcasing its adaptability and resilience, was converted from an industrial use to a commercial one. Wooden sidewalks were built, and this structure was renamed 'The Boardwalk'. The building was also used as a high school for many years until 2020.

Renovations were done in 1971 and 1986 when the back alley was closed, and the two buildings were connected with an atrium. More renovations started in 2019 and were completed in spring 2024. Today, this complex is called the Revillon Boardwalk Building, and both structures have received their historic designation by the city.

Borden Park

112 Avenue by 73 Street

Decades before Hawrelak Park was the best-known city park, there was Borden Park. Initially, this was mostly swamp land far outside the city limits. This park has been an essential attraction since it opened in 1906. At that time, it was called East End City Park, then it renamed for Robert Borden after he visited Edmonton in 1914 on the eve of the First World War. Borden served as Canada's eighth Prime Minister.

Up to seven thousand people would gather every Sunday for picnics, concerts, baseball, and a popular tea room. Starting in 1915, many other attractions were added, such as the fairgrounds, a carousel, a roller coaster, and a tunnel of love. One of the city's first three swimming pools was constructed in 1924, followed by Edmonton's first zoo in 1931. Most of those attractions disappeared over the next couple of decades.

The entire park was closed in the 1950s as part of a $100,000 improvement. A band shell was constructed in 1956, along with a new drainage system, sidewalks, and a picnic/sports area. The opening of the refurbished park was held on July 1, 1958, and it was a big event. Three thousand people turned out as Mayor Hawrelak gave a speech, and the Loyal Edmonton Regiment Band played in the new band shell, which has since been deemed a Municipal Historic Resource.

A facelift was planned in 2006 to protect and revitalize this place. The revitalization of Borden Park commenced in 2011. The natural swimming pool was the final piece completed in 2017. The public washroom here was a top-five finalist in 'Canada's Best Restroom Contest' in 2021.

Bowker Building

109 Street and 98 Avenue

Built in 1931, it was originally called the Administration Building. It was also known as the Natural Resources Building when the transfer of natural resources to provincial jurisdiction took place by the federal government. The building also housed the Attorney General's office, and in 1981, it was renamed the Bowker Building to honour Dr. Wilbur Fee Bowker's contributions to the legal profession. He was a University of Alberta graduate who practiced law for ten years before enlisting to fight in World War II. Upon returning home, he went on to head both the U of A law faculty and the Alberta Institute of Law Reform until he retired in 1975.

The Bowker Building, was to alleviate overcrowding at the Legislature and accommodate government offices scattered around the city, originally cost $940,000, it was heated by steam generated from an underground powerhouse. This majestic structure currently has no historical recognition.

Brintnell Neighbourhood

50 Street and 153 Avenue

It is named after Leigh Brintnell. His flying career started in 1917 when he joined the Royal Flying Corps. He received his Private Pilot's Licence and then became an instructor for pilots in World War I. After the war, Brintnell worked at a few aviation companies and owned some as well. Including Arctic Airlines, doing aerial photography, where he had his hand in discovering uranium from the photos he took of the odd land formations in the territories. He also helped start Canadian Pacific Airlines and a company called Aircraft Repair Limited at the City Centre Airport. He initially had twenty-four employees and grew to 1,750 by 1943. Brintnell even developed his own airplane called 'The Northwest Ranger.' He received many awards, including the Order of the British Empire in 1946. He was inducted as a Member of Canada's Aviation Hall of Fame in 1976.

Brownlee Building

97 Street and 103 Avenue

This 10-storey building was constructed in 1983 for several agencies and departments of the Government of Alberta. It is named after John Brownlee, who was Alberta's fifth Premier and is considered one of the best in the province's history. He was successful in negotiating the transfer of resource rights from the federal government to the province when he served from 1925 to 1934. John Brownlee is also known for holding the first driver's licence in the province in 1929.

Buena Vista Apartments

124 Street and 102 Avenue

This three-story red brick building was constructed in 1912 as an apartment and retail complex. A Grocery store was initially on the main level, but over the years, several other businesses, including a bank, several restaurants, and drugstores have occupied this space.

The ten apartments on the upper levels had hardwood floors, high ceilings, and natural gas fireplaces. It was one of the most desirable residential properties in the west end of downtown.

The most famous person who lived in this place was Wilfrid "Wop" May, a World War I ace and legendary bush pilot.

Although this place was not on the city's historic list, it remained and made part of the twenty-seven storey MacLaren Tower.

Calgary/Edmonton Railway Station Museum

86 Avenue and 105 Street

The original building was constructed in 1891 after the rail tracks were completed. It served as the north end of the line until 1907 when the station became too busy and too small. A larger station was built by Whyte Avenue and 103 Street. This structure was moved and turned into a house. It was moved again to this location in 1978 and fell into disrepair. In 1980, a partial replica was constructed to keep the history alive.

The rail line still exists, although train passenger service was discontinued in 1985. The Edmonton Radial Railway Society operates vintage street cars down this portion of the line from Old Strathcona, across the High-Level Bridge to downtown. This happens throughout the summer, starting on Victoria Day long weekend.

Calder Cenotaph

120 Street and 128 Avenue

At the time of the Second World War, Calder was a Village north of Edmonton before the city absorbed it. Calder residents wanted to honour nine individuals from the Village who died in the Second World War. This memorial was unveiled on November 6, 1949. Bronze plaques were also added to honour those who fought in the First World War and the Korean War.

The Calder Cenotaph is highly significant. It is one of only three war memorial cenotaphs in Edmonton, the others being in Beverly and at City Hall. Remembrance Day ceremonies have been held at this location since the 1970s.

On March 7, 2017, the City Council approved the designation of the Calder Cenotaph as a Municipal historic monument.

Calder School

118 Street and 129 Avenue

The area is named after Hugh and Sandy Calder, who purchased the land in 1912. The Calder neighbourhood was developed for railroad workers and their families after the arrival of the Grand Trunk Pacific Railway in 1909.

With a growing population, a larger school was needed to replace the original one that opened in 1907 and the second one that was constructed in 1911. Both were near this one, which was built in 1926. The school was heated by coal before a new boiler system was installed. Eight new classrooms were added in 1935, four more in 1950, and then a gymnasium in 1971.

To keep this place's history alive, the library has some of the school's first library books on the top shelves.

Cameron Block

97 Street and 105 Avenue

A building permit was issued on July 11, 1910, with the completion date later the same year. This two-storey brick building was constructed on a city's central business street. It was designed by architect J.H. Rudy, who arrived in Edmonton in 1909 and left the city in 1914 to fight in World War I. The first business was a drugstore on the main floor, with apartments on the second. An addition was built in the back at a later date. Over the years, as businesses came and went, this place became rundown and wasn't maintained. However, recognizing its historical and architectural significance, an application was sent to the city to protect it from demolition. The approval of its status as a municipal historic building was a victory for local heritage preservation.

Canada Consolidated Rubber Company Building

104 Street and 102 Avenue

Initially, the Kerr Building was located on this spot in 1912. It cost $55,000 to build, but a few months later, in January 1913, it burned to the ground. The land was purchased, and in just two months, a new warehouse was built at double the original cost of $110,000. Since 1913, it has been known as the Canada Consolidated Rubber Company Building. They made footwear, waterproof clothing, hoses, automobile and carriage tires.

This building served the rubber company until 1935. Other companies bought it, including Kaufman Rubber Company and the Army and Navy Department Store.

Following its rich history, the building has been restored and now serves a new purpose as the Cobogo Lofts and Condominiums.

This place received its municipal historic designation on November 27, 2001.

Canada Packers Smoke Stack

Fort Road and 125 Avenue

This part of north Edmonton was called Packingtown, referring to the four meat packing facilities, Swift's, Burns', Capital Packers, and Canada Packers, located here. Edmonton's stockyard became second in size only to Chicago's Union Stock Yards.

Construction on the plant started in 1936, and after laying 1.1 million bricks and pouring 14,000 tons of concrete, the building was completed in six months. This place included a power plant and a refrigeration plant, producing 50 tons of ice daily and was Western Canada's first vegetable oil refinery plant. The building won an architectural award for its design.

In the 1950s, 60s, and 70s, over one thousand people worked at the Canada Packers Plant every day. It closed in 1994 and was demolished, but the 40-metre smoke stack survived as a reminder of what was once here.

Canada Permanent Building

100 Street and 101 Avenue

The Canada Permanent Building started as the provincial headquarters of the Canada Permanent Mortgage Company and maintained this location for over 50 years. At the time, it was the oldest and largest loan institution in Canada.

The three-story building was built in 1910 for $65,000. At this branch, they dealt primarily with mortgages for farms, private residences, and small commercial ventures.

The Canada Permanent Building and the neighbouring McLeod Building were slated for demolition in 1980, but a public outcry led the provincial government to purchase both buildings.

Numerous plans have emerged to reuse the 3,200-square-foot space, which has sat empty for years. Most Edmontonians know this place as the original location of the Japanese Village restaurant, which occupied the building from 1974 to 2012. It was designated a Provincial Historic Resource in 1995.

Canadian Pacific Rail Station

Gateway Boulevard and 82 Avenue

CP built the original station in 1891, and it was quite small. As the demand grew for the number of people moving here, a larger station was needed, so this was constructed in 1908 for $24,000. The train crews used the upstairs as living quarters. The ground floor had all the essential amenities for the passengers at the time, such as separate waiting rooms for men and women and a smoking lounge.

It was called Strathcona Station until 1932, when it was changed to South Edmonton Station. It operated as that until 1985, when the last passenger train departed here.

Since 1998, the former station has been a nightclub, restaurant, and bar. The city and the province designated it historic in 2003.

Capitol Theatre

At Fort Edmonton Park

The original theatre location was on Jasper Avenue, east of 101 Street. It opened in 1918 and was called the Allen Theatre, Edmonton's first dedicated movie house. In 1923, Famous Players bought it and re-named it the Capitol Theatre. It was closed in 1929 for renovations. On the outside, an electric sign and marquee was installed. The construction of a balcony inside added 500 more seats; the walls and ceilings had antique gold, and a new sound system gave the moviegoer a better experience with the talking movies.

Another renovation was done in 1938, adding air conditioning and Canada's largest marquee vertical sign. It had 2000 60-watt bulbs, generating so much heat that it would melt the snow and ice off the sidewalk in front of the theatre. The Edmonton Symphony Orchestra used the Capitol Theatre as their first home from 1952 to 1957.

Chapman Brothers Building

82 Avenue and 104 Street

In 1907, Robert Ritchie, the owner of the Edmonton Milling Company, constructed this building. It was an outlet for the Great West Saddlery Company, which was managed by Archibald Benjamin Chapman. In 1912, it was renamed Chapman A.B. Company and then changed to Chapman Brothers once his sons became involved in the business, selling horse harnesses and leather goods.

As motor vehicles became more popular, the need for their products started to decline. They began to sell Western clothing and sublet parts of this structure to other businesses, including a cafe and the MacDonald Jewelry Store, which operated here from 1949 to 1973.

This place has had few changes over the years, but an overhaul was done in the 1980s. Removing the estimated 20-30 coats of paint from the facade took three weeks.

This place received its historic designation from the Province in 1976.

Chateau Lacombe Hotel

101 Street and Bellamy Hill

It is named after Father Lacombe, who was a Roman Catholic missionary. Construction of this nine million dollar building started in 1964, with an opening date two years later. It almost didn't happen, all because of a law dating back to 1933. It stated that the river bank land was to remain parkland. The city council decided that this area was not considered a part of the riverbank and that the project could proceed. There were plans to build a second tower, but the cost was too much just for the footings. So, just one tower is here, with 24 floors and 307 rooms, and it was one of the first hotels in the country to have air conditioning. There is a rotating restaurant at the top; it was the largest in the world; it takes 88 minutes for the restaurant to make one complete revolution.

The first guests to stay here paid $17 a night for their room; the most expensive shot of whiskey was $1.45. The first wedding reception in the ballroom cost $300, the equivalent of about $7200 today. The hotel has been sold a few times and had a few different names, such as the Holiday Inn and the Crowne Plaza, before coming full circle back to the Chateau Lacombe.

Churchill Wire Building

100 Street and 102 Avenue

Built in 1947, this two-and-a-half-storey building was constructed for Edmonton Telephones to house the large switching equipment necessary for telephone service. It played a crucial role in Edmonton's post-war expansion, as the city continued to grow and Edmonton Telephones needed more space. In 1958, a four-storey addition was added on the west side. This exchange needed thirty-six people to operate and manage the equipment. The building was used until 1984. It was vacated, and the telephone equipment was removed. The building was later redeveloped into apartments and then into a bank. There is no historical recognition of this place.

Civil Defence Bunker

Mackenzie Ravine and 142 Street

Built in 1953, this 2,600-square-foot underground structure was the front line of the city's civil defence. During the Cold War, Edmonton was believed to be a target of the Soviet Union, since we had oil refineries, so they wanted a command centre.

The shelter was not designed to withstand a bomb's impact; it was intended for up to 36 people who would coordinate the city's response and recovery.

This bunker never saw any use except for the staff practicing the emergency protocols.

Despite being sealed off, the city recognizes its significance and lists it as one of its historic properties. While there are no immediate plans for the site, a group advocates for its restoration and transformation into a museum. This move would preserve and respect the history of Edmonton's Civil Defence Bunker.

CJCA Radio Station

Edmonton's and Alberta's first radio station

The Edmonton Journal started broadcasting the radio station on May 1, 1922. They operated from the third floor of the Journal's building, with a fifty-watt signal. 1922 was a big year for radio in the country, as fifty-seven authorized stations hit the airwaves in Canada within a year, including CJCA. All private commercial broadcasting stations had to follow strict rules to get a licence. They had to have a four-letter call sign starting with "CF," "CH," "CJ," or "CK." Also, an additional "C" had to be the third or fourth letter. There were also some strange government rules that stations had to follow, including no direct advertising between 6:30 PM and 11 PM without written consent from the Minister of Marine and Fisheries.

CJCA broadcasted the Edmonton Eskimo football games for twenty-four years, as they aired more than five hundred consecutive games. After seventy-one years, the station briefly went off the air when it closed on December 1, 1993. New owners brought the station back to life on April 3, 1994.

Clarke Stadium

Stadium Road

It was named after Joseph Clarke, the city's 15th Mayor. Clarke's friend, Prime Minister Mackenzie King, deeded the land for a public sports area. The stadium opened in 1938 for the Edmonton Eskimos in the Western Interprovincial Football Union. That only lasted two seasons before they folded due to World War II. The cost of construction was $7000. It had a sitting capacity of 20,000, putting that into perspective, that was 22% of the city's population.

The Edmonton Eskimos once again called this home from 1949 to 1978. In that time, the team won five Grey Cups before moving to Commonwealth Stadium, where they won another nine cups in those years. After football moved from Clarke Stadium, this became home for the city's professional soccer teams, such as the Edmonton Drillers, the Brickmen, the Aviators and FC Edmonton, along with numerous amateur sports clubs and high school teams.

The majority of the facility was demolished in June 2000 to modernize and rebuild. The seating capacity has changed from the original 20,000 to 5,100. This stadium has also hosted concerts by the Tragically Hip, Midnight Oil, and Dolly Parton, all back in 1993.

Cloverdale Neighbourhood

95 Street and 97 Avenue

This area is where one of the earliest tent cities started. During the early 1900s, Edmonton experienced a rapid economic boom, leading to a housing crisis. The exorbitant cost of housing and its scarcity compelled a large number of people to adopt unconventional living arrangements. The situation was so dire that many residents had to resort to living in tent communities. A 1907 survey revealed that nearly 1100 tents were providing shelter to 3300 individuals, constituting a staggering 23 percent of the population. To put this into perspective, if a similar situation were to occur today, it would mean a staggering 230,000 residents living in tents.

Despite the challenging circumstances, many residents saw the potential prosperity this part of the province held and remained hopeful for better days. Tents, being a more affordable housing option than houses, were either self-made or purchased pre-sewn by many.

The city started regulating this community by passing a bylaw stating that people could live in tents if they paid their $1 licence fee. The health department would then be aware of them and enforce the local health code to prevent the spread of diseases such as typhoid.

By 1912, as more houses were being constructed, the population of tent cities dropped to 2600 occupants or five percent.

CN Tower

104 Avenue and 100 Street

The original Canadian National train station opened at this location in 1905. It was busy for many decades and became too small, so it was demolished in 1953. The grand opening ceremonies of this 26-storey building was a big deal when it opened on February 14, 1966. Lieutenant Governor Grant MacEwan and Premier Ernest Manning attended. That`s because this was the tallest building west of Toronto.

It would remain Western Canada's tallest building until 1971, when Edmonton House surpassed it on 100 Avenue, and the Alberta Government Telephones Building, now the Telus Tower. Even though the CN letters are still on the building, they moved out in 2008. In 2009, the exterior of the building was damaged by a severe thunderstorm, as the falling debris crushed a couple of vehicles parked below. The tower has been sold a couple of times, once in 2011 and again in 2020.

Commonwealth Stadium

Stadium Road and 112 Avenue

The stadium was built for the Commonwealth Games, which held the opening ceremonies on August 3, 1978. Construction started in the latter part of 1974, removing 380,000 cubic metres of dirt for the field to be lower than street level. The original cost of the 42,500-seat venue was $20.9 million, plus an additional $18.2M for the roof. The roof almost doubled the price, therefore it was opted to go without one. Queen Elizabeth and Prince Phillip, for the first time, officially opened the Commonwealth Games. There was even a royal throne constructed for them, as they had a private bathroom by their seats below field level. The Royals never used the facilities, but one person did, a six-year-old boy named Justin Trudeau. The Commonwealth Games have gone through a few name changes. 1930-1950, they were called 'The British Empire Games', then the 'British Empire and Commonwealth Games' until 1962. Then, the next 16 years, they were called 'The British Commonwealth Games' until the games were held here in 1978, then known as the 'Commonwealth Games.' That year, Canada was ranked number one in medals, with 45 gold, 31 silver, and 33 bronze for 109, followed by England with 87 medals. In total, 1,474 athletes and 504 officials from 46 Commonwealth countries participated.

Connaught Armoury

103 Street and 85 Avenue

This place was built in 1911 for $35,000. It was named for the Duke of Connaught, a son of Queen Victoria and Canada’s Governor-General from 1911 to 1916. This is the oldest existing armoury in the province. It had a large drill hall on the main floor, with storerooms for guns, saddles, and uniforms. The basement had a rifle range and a bowling alley for recreation. Soldiers were trained at this armoury and sent to war in 1914 and again in 1939. The building was an important facility serving Canada's Armed Forces until 1965.

It was threatened with demolition in the early 1970s but was sold to the city and designated a provincial historic site in 1979. Since then, it has been used for several businesses, including restaurants and nightclubs.

Corbett Hall

114 Street and 82 Avenue

When this structure was opened in 1930, its purpose was to train teachers, but during World War II, the South Wing was used as a Training School for the Royal Canadian Air Force. In 1954, it became home to training physical therapists and became the first institution in Canada to offer a graduate degree in physical therapy.

This place was re-named in 1963 as Corbett Hall, after Ned Corbett. He served as University Director and founder of Canada's first university radio station, CKUA, in 1927. Several faculties, including Education and the Drama Department, have used Corbett Hall. In 1988, this building was closed for an $11 million renovation and re-opened three years later. Corbett Hall is also home to the "Ghost of Emily." It dates back to the 1930s, and students today still say they see her walking across the stage in the building's auditorium.

Crawford Block

Gateway Boulevard north of 82 Avenue

Herbert Crawford came to Alberta from Ontario in 1898 to work as an auctioneer. He also made and sold tents, awnings, and mattresses before becoming a Member of the Provincial Legislature. Requiring more space for his business, he designed a three-storey building and had it constructed in 1912. Within a year, Crawford expanded the first floor by 6,000 square feet and added a large basement. In 1935, he sold the building, and Strathcona Furniture opened. It was a mainstay for over six decades before closing in 1996. Restoration took place to revive the old building. In 2016, the apartment block expanded to five floors to hold forty units, each around 400 square feet.

In 2014, the Crawford Block was rightfully recognized for its historical significance and designated as a Municipal Historic Resource.

Cromdale School

79 Street and 112 Avenue

Developer William Magrath paid the city $20,000 to extend a streetcar line to the Highlands area. The Rail line went along Jasper Avenue to 82 Street and then east on 112 Avenue, in front of the new Cromdale School that was completed in 1931.

The school, a cornerstone of the community, served generations of students until, like many other schools, it faced the issue of declining enrollment and closed its doors in 1980.

It was repurposed a few times, serving as Edmonton Immigrant Services, low-cost housing, and services for at-risk youth. Capital Health took over the property, which became part of the Eastwood Community Health Clinic in 2008.

Cy Becker Neighbourhood

167 Avenue and 50 Street

The city's Northeast is collectively known as Pilot Sound. This community received its name in 1981 as a reminder of our proud aviation history and will become one of seven neighbourhoods named after Edmonton pilots as they are developed. One is Cy Becker, by 50 Street between 167 Avenue and Anthony Henday Drive. It is named after Charles 'Cy' Becker, an aviation pioneer who served in the First World War with the Royal Naval Air Service. When he returned, he graduated from the University of Alberta with a law degree in 1923.

Becker was an active member of the Edmonton Flying Club; he helped establish the City Centre Airport, Commercial Airways Limited and the Northern Waterways Company, which provided transportation to the Mackenzie River. He is also in the history books for delivering the first airmail to remote northern communities. Through all that, he utilized his law degree as a crown prosecutor and was appointed to the Queen's Council.

Dawson Bridge

Rowland Road and 87 Street

Originally known as the East End Bridge, it was the second bridge to cross the North Saskatchewan River in the city when it opened in October 1912. It was built for $145,000 and designed for horse-drawn wagons and electric trains to the Dawson Coal Mine on the east side of the river. It was constructed to transport coal quicker into downtown for industry and home heating.

That happened for 32 years until the Dawson Mine was closed in 1944. The bridge was converted to carry vehicle and pedestrian traffic, which continues today.

Rehabilitation work has been performed on this bridge several times, most recently in 2010, and scheduled to be done again in 2025.

Delton Grocery Store

122 Avenue and 88 Street

Built in 1914, it was the cornerstone of the neighbourhood. When it opened, it was known as Delton Meat Market, but as time went on, additional products were added to make it a one-stop store for all your needs. This was the early version of a big box store, or in this case, a small neighbourhood store.

Over a century later, this place still functions as a grocery store. This type of local commercial store is rare in the city, as only a few remain. This building received its historic designation in 2019.

Derwas Apartment Building

121 Street and 101 Avenue

This place was built to help with the housing shortage, like many other apartments such as the Westminster, Annamoe, and the LeMarchand. This structure was completed in 1914, just two months before the First World War started. It was considered a very stylish place in the west end of downtown. Each floor had four suites, and each one had a fireplace in the living room, a balcony, a formal dining area, but a small kitchen and only a single bedroom.

With the city's strong growth at that time, the vacancy filled quickly.

This is a tough old building. In 2011, a fire broke out on a balcony. Quick actions from the firefighters got it under control, saving this historic building. Repairs were completed, and this place saw its 100th birthday and many more since.

Dickinsfield Neighbourhood

82 to 97 Streets and from 137 to 144 Avenue

This north Edmonton area is named after a famous local pilot, Clennell Haggerston Dickins. Or better known as Punch Dickins. He enlisted in World War I in the Canadian Infantry before transferring to the Royal Flying Corps to earn his pilot's wings. For his flying, he was awarded the Distinguished Flying Cross for his persistence and gallantry in completing aerial assignments while under fire. When Dickins returned to Canada, he became one of the original officers of the Royal Canadian Air Force, which had started in 1924. He conducted high-altitude experiments to prove that cold-weather flying was possible. He left the RCAF in 1927 to join the newly formed Western Canada Airways Ltd. and ran airmail flights across the prairies between Winnipeg and Edmonton. Dickins also aided in mapping much of the north; he flew by the position of the sun most of the time. That's because he only had a compass, which wasn't very reliable, and a map with the word "unexplored" printed across much of it. A twelve-day trip was a success, and Dickins was awarded the Trans-Canada Trophy for his outstanding contribution to Canadian aviation.

He joined de Havilland Aircraft as the Director and Vice President. The company unveiled a newly designed airplane called the 'Beaver', which would revolutionize bush flying. Then, he developed a worldwide sales organization that sold Canadian-designed and built aircraft in over 60 countries. When Dickins retired from flying, he travelled more than one million miles across the uncharted north, often in poor weather.

He was considered one of the most outstanding Canadians in this nation's first 100 years. Native groups gave him the names 'The Snow Eagle' and 'Canada's Sky Explorer'.

He was appointed an Officer of the Order of Canada for his service to the country and inducted as a Member of Canada's Aviation Hall of Fame.

In 2004, NASA's Mars Exploration Rover Project named a rock in the Endurance Crater "Punch Dickins Rock" to commemorate his flying.

Dominion Hotel

82 Avenue and 103 Street

Situated on Whyte Avenue, The Dominion Hotel is a beautiful four-storey structure built in 1903. It had thirty-three rooms, a dining room, a public bar, and a beer parlour to support those moving to the west. Things changed in 1916 when prohibition started. Sales of alcohol stopped, which saw the hotel close. The upper floors became rental units, and various businesses came and went on the main floor over the decades.

This place looks like it's from the Old West. With the second-floor balcony, you can imagine a shootout happening here.

The building is rich in history, as it received its historic designation in 1976.

Donald Ross School

101 Street and 97 Avenue

This place was built in 1913 for $34,000. The main floor had two classrooms and an assembly area. The second floor had three more classrooms and a staff room, with two vaults in the basement.

The school operated for 61 years before closing in 1974. Many groups have used the building, including the 1978 Commonwealth Games planning committee, the 2001 World Track and Field Games planning committee, the River Valley Outdoor Centre, and Edmonton Public Schools for Student Transportation. The treasured value of this school is recognized, which is why it is still standing, and the wrecking ball has yet to come for it.

Douglas Block

82 Avenue and 104 Street

In 1899, James and Robert Douglas started a small general store. They went on to establish one of Alberta's largest general mercantile stores.

The business was doing well, but the brothers had other interests. So they decided to get into real estate, and they built the Douglas Block in 1912. They never operated their store out of there; instead, they rented the main floor as retail space and the upper floors as apartments.

They both had public service on their minds. James became a Member of Parliament and the Mayor of Edmonton, while Robert was a School Board trustee and the Alberta Chief Liquor Vendor.

Many businesses have operated out of this building over the years and have continue to do so. This place received its historic designation in 1982.

Douglas Manor

108 Street and 83 Avenue

This place has quite a history; it was built around 1914. Initially, it was constructed as a rooming house, known as the Zelia Apartments. By 1919, it was converted to a seminary and re-named Neuman Hall, where university students lived. In the 1920s, it became the St. Mary's Home for Boys.

In 1942, it was sold and became Robert Mansion. After major renovations, it was converted back into apartments. In 1978, it was sold again and became known as Douglas Manor.

It has been empty for a few years, and renovations are taking place once again. This place received its municipal historic designation in 2019. A fire broke out in 2022, destroying much of the top floor.

E.L. Smith Water Treatment Plant

E.L. Smith Road

It was named after Eugene Lloyd Smith, the city's Chief Chemical Engineer from 1935 to 1960. Construction started in 1973, costing $21 million. It has been providing clean drinking water since 1976. Situated on a 75-acre site along North Saskatchewan River, the plant plays a crucial role in the region's water supply, producing 65 percent of the water for customers in the Edmonton region, with the remainder coming from the Rossdale Plant.

Initially, the water treatment capacity was over 151 million litres a day. As capacity grew, it now produces over 605 million litres per day. That became the largest individual treatment and softening plant in Canada.

This place has grown again with the solar farm construction that started in 2021. Forty-five thousand solar panels were installed, generating about twelve megawatts of energy to power the treatment plant. Any excess will be stored or put on the electrical grid.

Eastglen School

68 Street and 114 Avenue

This school opened in 1954 for $2.2 million. Additions happened in 1957 and again in 1961. Residents of the community selected the school's name since this was on the eastern edge of the city.

There was a shortage of school space in this part of the city in the 1950s, as the first 427 students started classes here before the official opening, which Premier Ernest Manning attended. Today, Eastglen is home to about 860 students.

Eastwood School

81 Street and 120 Avenue

This school was originally named after School Board Trustee Frank Scott. The first structure, a wood-frame school with only two rooms, was built in 1913 for $3800.

This is the second building on the current site. In 1914, the plan was for a seventeen room school, but work was delayed due to the First World War. Once the war was over, construction re-started and finished in 1922. In 1925, the residents petitioned for the school to be renamed after the area. They were successful, and this became Eastwood School. A third floor was added with nine additional rooms, and then enrollment was expanded to accept high school students.

Eastwood was the blueprint for several other schools in the city, such as Riverdale, built in 1923, Oliver and Spruce Avenue, built in 1928, and Cromdale in 1931.

Almost a century later, with a diminishing enrollment, the school closed in 2010. The building has been used by others, including Alberta Justice and Solicitor General, as a training centre and is now a private school called The Nebula Academy.

Edmonton Brewing and Malting Company Building

121 Street and 105 Avenue

It was built in 1913, at a cost of $250,000, by William Sheppard, a brewer and former mayor of Strathcona. It was constructed to replace their smaller brewery, originally located in the Rossdale neighbourhood. It was built here because it was beside a major roadway and rail line, which made it perfect for shipping their products.

It was a successful business until 1927 when it was sold to Fritz Sick, known for his Pilsner Beer. He sold it to Molson's in 1958. They operated until it was closed in 2007, marking the end of beer-making at this location after 94 years.

A portion of the brewery was torn down to create the Brewery District shopping area, which opened in 2016. That same year, the original building received its Municipal Historic designation.

Edmonton Cenotaph

At City Hall

As the First World War erupted in 1914, Edmonton's population stood at 72,516. Sixteen thousand of them bravely left Canada to fight, and three thousand never returned. Despite numerous failed attempts and fundraising efforts, a war monument remained elusive. It was the unwavering determination of A.E. Nightingale, a veteran himself, that finally saw the project through. In 1935, he initiated a fundraising campaign, requesting one dollar a month until the necessary funds were raised. In May 1936, veterans volunteered to construct the Cenotaph, a towering structure standing at twenty-three feet and weighing over one hundred tons. The historic unveiling happened on August 13, 1936, witnessed by a gathering of fifty-five hundred Edmontonians.

The Cenotaph, a symbol of Edmonton's wartime sacrifices, was initially located in a park behind the Edmonton Journal Building on 100 Avenue and 102 Street. In a significant move that underscored its growing importance, it was relocated to City Hall Plaza in 1978.

On December 7, 2021, the Cenotaph was declared a historic resource.

Edmonton Golf & Country Club

Country Club Road

When this place started in 1913, there were about 400 members before declining to 96 four years later, due to World War I. The annual fee to golf here was $15.00 for men and $5.00 for women, with green fees at $1.00 per day. But money was tight for the Club; the golf pro was also the groundskeeper. He was owed back pay and was given the Club's two cows for payment.

To earn extra income, the Club grew and sold hay. 1918 was the Club's lowest point, as the lower nine had been closed due to lack of membership and to help reduce maintenance costs. It rebounded in 1919, as the Prince of Wales, Edward the 8th, visited Edmonton and golfed here.

Prohibition was still happening during the tournament. A member of the club produced two cases of contraband Irish whisky, and the party was on. The road accessing the Club was always a problem when it rained; it stranded the golfers and forced them to stay the night. It was not until 1925 that the road was finally gravelled, mainly at the ladies' insistence.

A suspension bridge was added in the 1930s. One member jumped off of it, all for a $5 bet. The Second World War was painful for the Club, as members dropped out to join the war efforts again, leaving the Club with only 125 members. Everything was scarce; liquor and food were rationed, and gas was expensive. Oil exploration was done on the property; it's uncertain if any was discovered. The Clubhouse was a victim of an armed robbery in 1951. A new Clubhouse opened in 1956, and the Canadian Amateur Men's Championship, a prestigious event, was held here in 1961, bringing honour and prestige to the Club.

It's worth noting that drinking water had to be brought in by truck until the 1980s when a city water line was finally connected. Today, the Edmonton Country Club continues to be a thriving and integral part of the community.

Edmonton Motors Building

Jasper Avenue and 115 Street

In 1925, Edmonton Motors started as a dealership, selling 325 new vehicles in its first three months. They moved a couple of times before finding their home on Jasper Ave in 1951. An estimated 40,000 people showed up for the grand opening. For decades, the business has gone well at this location, even offering registry services for vehicles, the only auto dealership to do so in the city.

However, in 2019, after a remarkable 94-year journey, a new chapter began as Edmonton Motors transitioned to the west end, now operating under the name Wolfe Cadillac.

Today, this property is rezoned and waiting for two condominium towers to be built.

Edmonton Electric Lighting and Power Company

December 22, 1891, was a big day for electrification in the city. It was the day electric lights were turned on for the first time. It all started two months earlier with a group of entrepreneurs obtaining a permit to build the power company. They installed power poles along Jasper Avenue from 96 to 103rd Street and flicked the switch on. They only operated the company for eleven years before the Town of Edmonton bought the Electric Light & Power Company for $13,500 and became Canada's first municipally owned electric utility.

In 1905 round-the-clock electric service began, as the Light Department only had 53 customers. That same year, as Alberta became a province, Edmonton Power celebrated by giving customers free power for a week! As the city grew, so did the number of roads and vehicles. Traffic signals were needed, and the first one was installed in 1933.

Today, Edmonton has roughly 50,000 wooden power poles, which are inspected every five years for rot and damage. These poles are part of Alberta's 13,000 kilometres of power lines and 300 substations.

Eric Cormack Hospital & Natural Resource Building

98 Avenue and 112 Street

This part of downtown is owned by the province as the square block once had the original Misericordia Hospital. It still has the former home to the Colonel Eric Cormack Hospital, a powerhouse, and the Energy and Natural Resource Building, all constructed in the 1930s and 40s. The hospital is named after Eric Cormack, who served in both World War I and World War II in the Royal Canadian Artillery. Later, he became well-known for his work supporting the mentally ill.

The powerhouse has an underground tunnel from the hospital that the nurses used to sneak out of to go "dancing with the gentleman"!

The Energy and Natural Resource Building housed the province's offices before they re-purposed them.

These buildings do not have any historical recognition, and this piece of land is for sale. The site has been unoccupied since 2012, and it costs Alberta taxpayers more than $70,000 a year just for maintenance and security.

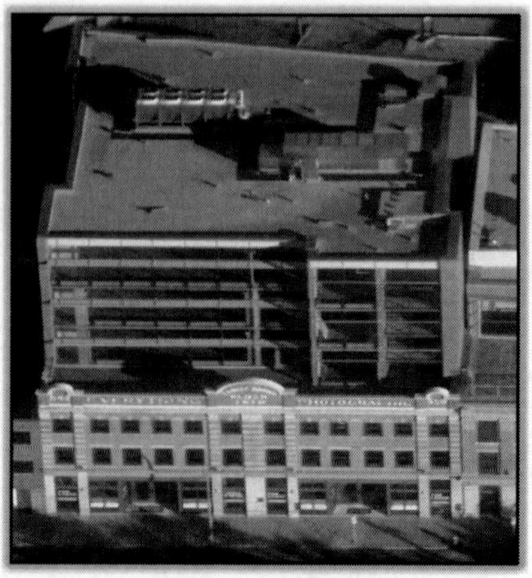

Ernest Brown Block

Jasper Avenue and 96 Street

Many of these historic buildings were part of the city's first development boom before the First World War. 1912 was a busy construction year in Edmonton, and this is another one built that year.

This three-storey structure was built for Ernest Brown, Edmonton's leading photographer at the time. It cost about $30,000 to construct and was to house his studio and historic photographic collections.

Brown did an incredible amount of business. In March 1914, the price tag of his assets was listed at $265,000. He would photograph buildings, streetscapes, and events in and around Edmonton.

In 1947, the provincial government recognized the value of his collection and purchased it along with his photo equipment and artifacts for $50,000. In later years, they would account for the most valued photographic collection in the Provincial Archives.

Fast-forward to the 2010s, this iconic structure underwent a transformation, adding three more floors and a mix of retail and office space. It was declared a Municipal Historic Resource in 2001.

Edmonton Transit's Buses

What does ETS stand for? Well, it depends on what year you are referring to. Before ETS was founded in 1908, it was the Edmonton Radial Railway. In 1946, it was renamed the Edmonton Transportation System; a year later, on April 29, 1947, it was known as the Edmonton Transit System. In 1976, it was referred to as Edmonton Transit. That lasted forty-one years until 2017 when another name change happened, and now it is known as the Edmonton Transit Service. Their logo has changed as many times as their name. ETS has preserved a large fleet of historic vehicles throughout all that. The oldest is from 1932, and the newest is from 2013, everything from conventional buses, trolleybuses, and a tow truck.

Federal Building

107 Street and 99 Avenue

The Federal Building, a ten-story architectural wonder, was designed in 1939 to consolidate Edmonton's federal employees. However, the outbreak of the Second World War led to a construction delay, and the building was not completed until the 1950s. One of its most distinctive features is the display of all ten Coats of Arms of each province, a testament to Canada's unity, along with a massive Canadian Coat of Arms above the main entrance, weighing four and a half tons and measuring about nine feet square. This place was finally unveiled in 1958 by Prime Minister John Diefenbaker.

After serving as a federal office for thirty years, the province acquired it in 1983 for $20.5 million. It lay dormant until 2010, when a series of extensive upgrades were undertaken to breathe new life into this architectural gem, now a vital part of the Legislature complex. On August 5, 2022, the Government of Alberta, in a significant move, received permission from Buckingham Palace to rename the structure as the Queen Elizabeth II Building, in honour of the Queen's Platinum Jubilee, marking seventy years of service. Sadly, she passed away thirty-four days later, on September 8.

Fire Hall #1

83 Avenue and 103 Street

The hall opened in 1910 for $15,000. Since the original fire engines were horse-drawn, the hall was designed to house the engines, a stable for the horses, and a dormitory for the firemen.

The fire hall's tower is 77 feet high and was one of the tallest structures in town. It was used to dry the hoses and house the alarm bell. It was decommissioned in 1954 and leased out as a furniture store for 20 years.

In 1974, it was transformed into the Walterdale Playhouse Theatre. It has been a theatre longer than a Fire Hall.

It was designated a Provincial Historic Building in 1976 and a Municipal one in 2011.

Fire Hall #7

118 Avenue and 65 Street

The City needed a fire hall in northeast Edmonton for years, and they finally built one in 1941. When Station Number 7 opened, the cost was $11,000. It was completely different from other fire halls in the City. It didn't have a second storey, which meant it didn't need the classic brass fire pole that firefighters used to quickly slide down to get to the trucks.

This new style of fire hall was manned by five firefighters, who managed a ladder truck and two pumps. The hall was big enough to store the Police Department's motorcycles.

As the northeast side of the City kept growing, they built a bigger fire station, so this place was closed in 1975, with the new Station 7 opening east of here at 50th Street. The City sold the old hall, and a number of different businesses have occupied the space over the years. Currently, it is home to a specialty butcher shop.

First Presbyterian Church of Edmonton

105 Street 100 Avenue

The initial meeting for this congregation was held on November 3, 1881. A year later, the first building opened at 104 Street and 99 Avenue. The second structure opened in 1902 at 103 Street and Jasper Avenue. This version opened in November 1912 with a seating capacity of over 1,200 people. The original estimate for construction was $85,000. The final cost was $170,000.

This is the largest Presbyterian church in Edmonton. The organ was originally built in 1909 and modernized in 1951. In 2004, another renovation was needed, so they began a $300,000 fundraiser for the project, and by mid-2007, the organ renovation was complete. They have hosted multiple concerts showcasing the organ. In September 1978, the building received its historic designation by the province and by the city in 2000.

Floden Park

111 Avenue and 42 Street

This park is named after Charles Floden, who moved to Alberta in 1908, west of Leduc, where he was offered 160 acres of land for $10. He stayed there until 1912 before moving to the Town of Beverly. He became a steelworker and worked construction on the High Level Bridge. When the bridge was completed, he served the community on the School Board for three terms, then as Town Councillor for one term and then as Mayor of Beverly for three terms until he retired in 1957. The residents petitioned the council to name a park after him for everything he did for this area. That happened in 1959 when this park bared his name, just one block from his home. Charles passed away in 1960 after a lengthy illness. From this park, you have a great view of the sun setting over the river and behind the city's skyline.

Freemason's Masonic Hall

100 Avenue and 103 Street

A century ago, it was common to belong to a club or organization. When this place opened in 1931, one in twelve Edmontonians were Freemasons. The construction cost was $170,000, which was a lot of money at the time, considering it was the Great Depression.

The exterior design has a Gothic and medieval appearance. On the inside, they have the oldest working passenger elevator in the province. The shovel used for the ground-breaking ceremony in 1930 with many of the original hand-drawn blueprints hang on the walls throughout the building.

This four-storey building looks small from the outside, but on the inside, the main floor has an auditorium that holds two hundred people, office space, and remnants of the city's first lending library.

The basement has a banquet space for up to one hundred and fifty people, a lounge, and a commercial kitchen. On the upper floors, two lodge rooms with stained glass windows are still used to hold their meetings. They have plenty of detailed hand-crafted woodwork.

Gainer Block

82 Avenue and 103 Street

It was constructed in 1893 by John Gainer, who owned Gainer Meats. He played a prominent role in developing the livestock marketing industry in Western Canada.

Initially, the Gainer Block was built with a wood frame, but in 1902, a by-law required brick construction to reduce the risk of fires. After the rebuild, this was the second brick building on Whyte Avenue.

The main floor was the butcher shop until 1911, when it changed to retail and office space. As the business grew, the Gainers moved to a larger facility, and the building was sold in 1943. Since then, several companies have come and gone. Over 130 years later, this place is still an essential historical building in Old Strathcona, as it received its historical designation in 1982.

Gariepy Mansion

99 Avenue and 104 Street

Joseph Gariepy moved to Edmonton from Quebec in 1892 at the age of forty. He was a founding member of the Edmonton Board of Trade, an Alderman, a school board trustee, and a businessman. In 1898, Gariepy started a general store and made his fortune by outfitting gold-seekers on their way to the Klondike. Then, he turned his attention to real estate.

Joseph Gariepy, in need of more living space, commissioned the construction of this mansion in 1903. In 1923, he sold it to John A. McDougall, who, a year later, transformed it into Rosary Hall, a mission dedicated to supporting single women in need. That continued for 88 years until 2012.

This grand mansion remains one of the few early ones in Edmonton. It does not have any historic recognition.

Garneau Neighbourhood

Saskatchewan Drive to University Avenue

After participating in the Louis Riel Rebellion in Manitoba in 1870, Laurent Garneau moved to Edmonton in 1874 with his wife Eleanor and their nine children. He became this area's first resident, and the community was named after him when Edmonton's population was just one hundred. He sold all the things one would need at the time: land, coal, wood, fur, and food.

Also, in 1874, the Garneau's planted a Manitoba Maple tree on 111 Street by 90 Avenue. This was the first recorded tree planted in the city. The tree stood there for 143 years before coming down in 2017.

After his death in 1924, many buildings were named to honour Garneau, including a theatre, school, Community League and an apartment tower that was the area's first high-rise in 1963.

Garneau Park

109 Street and 83 Avenue

Harry Ainlay, the principal of the nearby Garneau School, convinced the city to allow this piece of land for recreation. The tennis courts have been here since 1926.

It started with four shale tennis courts constructed by volunteers. A small clubhouse and a skating rink were built a year later. In 1929, the Garneau Community League Tennis Club started as the club operated this facility. Over the next several decades, additional tennis courts were built, along with a multi-use building, which included squash and racquetball courts. There was also a lawn bowling green and beach volleyball courts.

The new City Arts Centre opened in the building in 2000, and for its 90th anniversary in 2016, money was raised to install new lights on the tennis courts.

Garneau Theatre

109 Street and 87 Avenue

Constructed in 1940, the theatre features 300 seats on its main level and a 200-seat mezzanine level. It was named after Laurent Garneau, who arrived in Edmonton in 1874 and began his career as an entrepreneur, selling wood, coal, land, fur, and food.

The Garneau Theatre was the second cinema built outside the downtown core, the first being the Roxy Theatre on 124th Street. The Garneau still operates as a theatre and a long-standing local landmark. A year later, in 1941, it was leased to Famous Players, who continued to operate the theatre until 1990. Magic Lantern Theatres took over the lease until June 2011, when the local non-profit Metro Cinema Society operated it. In 2009, the building underwent an extensive restoration to make the theatre look like it did in the 1940s.

General Hospital

Jasper Avenue and 111 Street

The Edmonton General opened in 1896 as the first hospital in the city. The Sisters of Charity of Montreal, also known as the Grey Nuns, started what some said to be the best medical care in Edmonton.

The General was the largest facility, with 36 beds on three floors, including an operating theatre, employee quarters, and isolation rooms. The land also contained a small farm with 'hospital' cows that provided food. The construction cost was a massive $30,000.

As the city grew, so did the hospital. Expansions happened in 1907, 1921, 1940, and again in 1951.

The hospital served downtown until 1989 when the acute care beds were transferred to the new Grey Nuns Hospital in Millwoods. This place is still open and adapting to the city's needs. Currently, they offer Continuing Care, long-term care, and hospice services.

Gibbard Block

112 Avenue and 64 Street

This three-story building, constructed in 1912 at a cost of $90,000, housed luxury apartments in the newly developed Highlands district.

The building originally featured nine suites on the second and third floors and a grocery and drug store at street level. Ahead of its time, each suite had electric lighting, its own telephone and intercom, hot water in bathrooms, and a central gas plant that provided fuel for cooking.

Due to a financial collapse in 1926, Queen's University in Kingston, Ontario, became the owner of the Gibbard Block since they held the mortgage on the property. The university sold it in 1945. As time ticked on, the building changed hands several times, and by the 1970s and 80s, it served as low-income housing.

In 2018, The Gibbard Block underwent a $2.5 million renovation, which transformed it to its original elegance. In 1992, it was designated a registered Provincial historic resource, marking a new chapter in its history.

Gibson Block

Jasper Avenue, 96 Street, and 101A Avenue

Realtor William Gibson built this place in 1913. It has four storeys to this flatiron design, noticeable in the distinctive triangular building shape. This was a popular method of developing properties previously considered unusable. It remains Edmonton's only flatiron building. The Gibson Block originally had retail space on the main floor, offices on the upper floors and Turkish Baths in the basement until 1978. The office spaces were later converted to apartments. After many years of neglect, the Gibson Block was completely restored in 1994 to house the Women's Emergency Centre. This building was designated a Provincial Historic Resource in 1995.

Glenora School

135 Street and 102 Avenue

This school opened on November 14, 1940. It was considered one of the finest and most up-to-date schools and only the second in the city built during the Second World War. It costs $55,000 to construct the four classrooms, work room, staff room, and clinic. It also had an auditorium and two other rooms in the basement. The first year the school was open, three teachers taught 100 children. However, due to the baby boom, four more classrooms were needed and added to the back of the school in 1949. The original gym was converted to a library in the 1950s, and a new gymnasium was built on the north side in the 1960s.

Glenora Substation

Stony Plain Road and 135 Street

Constructed in 1956, the Glenora Substation was a unique architectural marvel, a departure from the typical blockhouse design in local power stations. Its most striking feature was the large plate glass windows, which offered a clear view of the building's interior. Although the work area's plate glass remains, they have been covered, regrettably obstructing the view of the power equipment.

Only some people were fans of the new design. The Glenora Substation design sparked outrage from the Edmonton Property Owner's Association. In May 1957, they decried the extravagance of the material used, such as the plate glass and terrazzo floors and the cost.

Gold Bar Wastewater Treatment Plant

50 Street and 109 Avenue

Since its inception in 1956, the Gold Bar Wastewater Treatment Plant has been a cornerstone of the city's development. Initially designed to serve a population of 250,000, the plant has grown in tandem with the city's expansion. Today, it can handle water treatment for about 900,000, treating 375 million litres of liquid and about 100,000 kilograms of solids daily. If it goes down the drain, it ends up here.

Sewage flows into the Gold Bar treatment plant and, after an initial round of treatment, is piped to Clover Bar, where it is processed and turned into fertilizer. This innovative process significantly reduces the amount of phosphorous that would otherwise end up in the North Saskatchewan River. Approximately 90% of the water that goes down your drain is returned to the river, a testament to our city's commitment to sustainability.

Goodridge Block

Jasper Avenue and 97 Street

This building opened in 1912. The upper floors were offices, while the main floor was home to many commercial businesses for the first couple of decades, such as a menswear store, barbershop, wine, liquor and cigar store, and pool hall.

In 1932, the main floor of the building was occupied by W.W. Sales Hardware, so Edmontonians knew this place as the W.W. Arcade Building.

The name lasted until they closed their doors in 1991. The Edmonton Downtown Business Corporation received funding from the federal government to restore the Goodridge Block. The grand reopening occurred in 1993, when it received its historic designation. The neon sign that was on the corner of the building for six decades lives on at the Neon Sign Museum on 104 Street south of Rogers Place.

Gorman Industrial Park

153 Avenue and Manning Drive

This area is named after George Gorman, who moved to Edmonton in 1906 and joined the Royal Air Force in 1916 to serve as a pilot in World War I. In 1918, Gorman was on a mission to destroy a bridge when he was shot down. He was a prisoner of war for only three months, as he was released when the war ended. Gorman returned to Edmonton as a barnstormer, entertaining crowds across the prairies. In 1921, he was among the first to fly into the Northwest Territories, following the Mackenzie River to Fort Norman for a new oil discovery.

He became friends with Wop May, and together they started a company called May-Gorman Airplanes Limited. Gorman was the first pilot to fly a commercial flight in western Canada. One of his regular flights was to fly the Edmonton Journal newspapers 45 miles to readers in Wetaskiwin.

Government House

102 Avenue and 128 Street

Completed in 1913, as the official residence for Alberta's Lieutenant Governor. It was not just a building but a witness to numerous important political and social events, hosting dignitaries and shaping history. From 1913 to 1938, it was home to six Lieutenant Governors.

Northwest Airlines leased the mansion during the Second World War and used it as office space and accommodations for personnel of the Northwest Staging Route.

Near the war's end, the building became a recovery hospital for wounded soldiers and later a veterans' home. In 1964, the Province reacquired the building and its grounds as the site for the Provincial Museum and Archives.

The building was renovated and reopened in 1976 as a government conference and meeting centre.

Grace Lutheran Church

114 Street and 99 Avenue

The history of the Lutheran faith in the city dates back to 1924. Lutheran services in Edmonton were usually conducted in German or Scandinavian languages. Services were held at multiple locations, including the Howard and McBride Funeral Home. The congregation united in their desire for a permanent home, purchased this land, and approved a $100,000 construction budget. Shovels were in the ground on August 22, 1954. The church was opened and dedicated on July 3, 1955. The final cost of construction came in at $118,429. Edmonton already had six other Lutheran churches, but this was the first to have services in English. The lots around the church were also purchased for expansion, one in 1963 and the adjacent lot in 1965.

Grand Hotel

103 Street and 103 Avenue

It was built in stages starting in 1904. As one of Edmonton's oldest hotels, it went from a great, affordable hotel for those who helped construct the city to a rundown relic and then back to a prospering hotel.

Although the 71 rooms are small, they remain the same size they have been for generations.

The new owners of the Grand Hotel, in their commitment to preserving the history, have spared no expense. They have invested a substantial $30,000 per room in upgrades, ensuring the hotel retains its unique character.

The Grand Hotel now has a new name, The Crash Hotel. It caters to a new clientele looking for that diamond in the ruff in the city centre.

Graphic Arts Building

Jasper Avenue by 95 Street

Built in 1913, the first known business to be located inside was a tin smith company. By the 1930s, the building was upgraded and modernized as a graphic arts and photography studio. In the latter days of the building, it was a recording studio and a tattoo parlour. However, as the decades passed, maintenance slipped, and the structure fell into despair. The city bought the building in 2015 and announced it would be demolished. A couple of groups approached the city to either purchase or move the front part of the building to a new location to preserve the Art Deco design. In the end, the city did tear it down in 2022 to use the land as a supply area for the nearby LRT construction.

Great Western Garment Company Building

97 Street and 103 Avenue

GWG was a garment company established on January 30, 1911, by three businessmen, including Alberta's first Premier, Alexander Rutherford. The shop produced workwear and military clothing. This building was initially constructed as a department store in 1911 but changed to a factory in 1914. The workforce started with one and fifty employees, primarily women, and grew to five hundred by 1939. Business was thriving, leading to the addition of two more floors in 1940.

They remained here until 1953, when another move occurred. Then, this place became home to the Army & Navy Department Store for the next few decades. The building was also home to the Downtown Farmers Market.

The Great Western Saddlery Company Building

104 Street and 101 Avenue

The Edmonton Saddlery Company started in 1886. It only lasted fourteen years before the Great Western Company from Winnipeg bought it.

This 45,000-square-foot warehouse opened in 1911 at a cost of $100,000. It employed thirty people providing leather goods such as jackets, bags, harnesses, and saddles. By the end of World War I in 1918, it was the largest saddlery company in the world.

As the horse and buggy faded away, they expanded into automobile accessories. However, as time passed, many of their products became obsolete, and the company went out of business. They owned this building until 1958, and over a century later, the ghost signs on both sides of the building are still visible, reminding us of this vital business that helped build the West.

Grierson Centre

101 Avenue and 95 Street

The original building opened in 1912 as the Northwest Mounted Police Barracks, costing $70,000; it is a two-storey L-shaped structure resembling a fortified castle. There was housing for five sergeants and twenty constables, and the facility contained thirteen jail cells. In 1932, the Royal Canadian Mounted Police replaced the provincial police force, and the barracks were expanded to accommodate extra officers. A new L-shaped addition was built on the west side in 1935. A third L-shaped addition on the east side was done in 1955 and constructed on the site of the old horse stables. The R.C.M.P. moved to their new offices on 109 Street and Kingsway Avenue in 1975. The barracks, now known as Grierson Centre, have since been used by the Correctional Service of Canada as the parole office and the Stan Daniels Healing Centre.

The first building received its federal heritage designation in 1985.

H. A. Gray School

103 Street and 121 Avenue

The school opened in 1914, costing just over $158,000. It had sixteen classrooms, each capable of holding forty-two students, for a total enrollment of 672. Like so many of the schools built at that time, it was on the edge of the city.

Named after Henry Allan Gray, an Anglican Bishop, a Public School Board Trustee and a Provincial Judge.

The sidewalks were wooden boardwalks, and the streets were ungraded trails.

Over the years, H. A. Gray School has undergone significant changes. It served the community for seventy years until its closure in 1984. After that, it transformed into the Westwood Campus of NAIT. Since 2004, it has been the home of Vanguard College, offering diploma and degree programs in Christian education, showcasing its resilience and commitment to education.

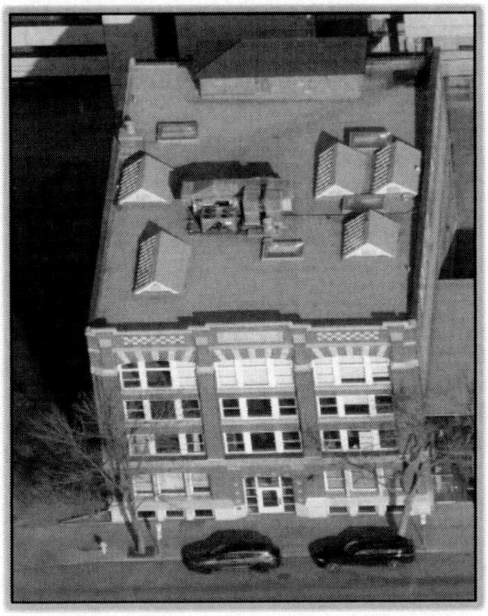

H.V. Shaw Building

105 Street and 102 Avenue

Built in 1914 as a cigar factory, this four-and-a-half-storey warehouse and office building was located on the edge of Edmonton's warehouse district.

Harry Shaw was one of Edmonton's early entrepreneurs and one of the city's largest employers. He started a cigar business in 1901, with his brands available across the prairies. The company grew to the point where he hired one of the city's largest crews of skilled labourers. By 1917, ninety people worked in the factory, producing over a million cigars yearly. Economic setbacks, prohibition, and the closing of saloons affected his business.

Over the years, the building has seen many different occupants. In 2002, a steel and glass addition was built on the south side to accommodate the Yellowhead Brewery. The building received its municipal historic designation in 2001.

Hangar 11

109 Street and 117 Avenue

Hangar 11, which significantly impacted the Second World War, was constructed by the United States government in 1942. It was built here for its location. With Edmonton having the only municipal airport in Canada, there were local people with technical know-how to support the movement of U.S.-built planes and equipment as they ventured to the Soviet Union to battle against Germany. Construction was rushed and hectic as there were no detailed drawings to go by, but this hangar was completed in just a few months.

Between 1942 and 1946, Edmonton witnessed an influx of 50,000 American Servicemen. In 1943, the volume of freight passing through Edmonton in a single week surpassed that of the entire year of 1939, a testament to the scale of the operation.

The United States delivered 14,000 aircraft to the Soviet Union, and more than 7,900 flew through this airport. The Americans transformed Blatchford Field, the airport's original name, into the busiest airport on the continent. One day in June 1942, five hundred planes took off for Alaska. On another day, eight hundred and sixty planes landed here. After the war, the hangar sat empty for several years, then re-purposed for civil aviation. Proposed plans happened to make the hangar into commercial space, but sadly, on April 22, 2024, the hangar was destroyed by an arson fire.

Hawrelak Park

Groat Road and 93 Avenue

The Strathcona Land Syndicate owned this land before it was a park. From 1911 to 1912, the city's population doubled, so they planned to develop the area into a residential subdivision with five hundred houses. Then, a real estate crash happened in 1913, and Strathcona Land forfeited its taxes. The city took over the land in 1922, and over the next thirty-two years, the city used the land as a garbage dump and then for gravel pit operation. In 1954, a park was proposed, and work began five years later, starting with the construction of a man-made lake.

Originally named Mayfair Park, it was officially opened on Canada Day in 1967 to celebrate the country's centennial. It kept that name for eight years until the City Council voted to rename this river valley gem after former mayor William Hawrelak.

Hecla Block

95 Street and 101 Avenue

John Johnson was a builder responsible for almost seventy houses and apartment blocks in the city for nearly twenty-five years. He emigrated to Canada with his family from Iceland and started with this place in 1914. It was named after Mount Hecla, Iceland's largest and most famous volcano, which last erupted in 2000. The building initially had seven one-bedroom suites per floor. It was one of the first apartment buildings in the city without commercial space on the main floor.

In 1924, Molson's Bank foreclosed on the building. The Edmonton Lands Company owned it for about fifty years.

The Hecla Block changed hands several times and was declared unfit for living. A fire in 1994 destroyed the interior. Renovations brought the building back to life. It now has fourteen apartment-style condominiums, celebrating a hundred and ten years in the city. This place received its Municipal Historic Resource in 1999.

High Level Bridge

109 Street over River Valley Road

It was one of the largest bridges in the West at 2,550 feet in length and 156 feet in height. It is mile zero of the Alaska Highway.

Construction took place from 1910 to 1913. The final cost was about $2,000,000.

The bridge was unique for the variety of traffic it carried. It had rail and streetcar traffic on the upper deck and two-way traffic for automobiles and pedestrians below. The last streetcar ran over the bridge on September 1, 1951. Rail passenger service across the bridge ended on October 28, 1972. In 1980, vehicle traffic became one-way southbound. Canadian Pacific stopped running freight trains in 1989.

1980 saw some pumps, pipes, and sprinklers on the bridge's east side form a vast waterfall called the Great Divide Waterfall. It was occasionally turned on in the summer for celebrations such as Canada Day. The waterfall was decommissioned in 2009. In 2015, 60,000 LED bulbs were installed due to the Light the Bridge Campaign. The bridge lights illuminate every night, featuring particular colours on specific dates to recognize significant events and cultural celebrations.

The High Level Bridge received its municipal historic designation in 1995.

Highlands School

62 Street and 118 Avenue

Construction started on Highlands in 1914, a twin to King Edward Park School in Old Strathcona. World War I interrupted the work, which delayed completion until 1920. The total cost was just over $210,000.

In the 1920s, it became the first teacher training institute in Alberta. An assembly hall was added in 1946, with six new classrooms in 1954 and more upgrades in 1977. The main facade has remained relatively unchanged over the past century.

In 2019, Highlands School underwent significant changes. The 1954 addition was demolished, and a new wing was constructed. This transformation reflects the school's evolution into a Kindergarten to Grade Nine facility, as it welcomed students from Mount Royal Elementary and Montrose Elementary, which closed in June 2021.

HMCS Nonsuch Building

Kingsway and 118 Street

The United States government constructed this place during World War II as a recreation centre. Inside, they had a bowling alley and a swimming pool, considered the first indoor pool in Alberta.

The Royal Canadian Navy took this place over in 1974 and renamed it HMCS Nonsuch. The name comes from a Hudson Bay ship that visited Fort Edmonton to collect beaver pelts. When you think of the Navy, most people don't think of the prairies, but there are seven Navy recruitment centres across the West. There are a total of twenty-four naval reserve units from coast to coast. The Nonsuch unit was founded in 1923 as a Royal Canadian Naval Volunteer Reserve half-company.

Today, there is plenty of office space; the hangar is the marching hall for the cadets, and the swimming pool is a dive tank for water training. Unlike the army, where soldiers are deployed as a unit, the Navy reserves train and deploy members as individuals. There are fifteen trades taught at Nonsuch; even though the sailors are a part of the Navy, they may participate in any operations run by the Canadian Armed Forces if they so choose. Built in 1942, this structure is still known as Building 42. If you are considering a job career in the forces, this is where you need to come to get the information.

Hollick-Kenyon Neighbourhood

50 Street and 153 Avenue

Named after Herbert Hollick-Kenyon, born in London, England, in 1897, moved to British Columbia, and at seventeen, joined the Canadian Army as a trooper, then was sent overseas to fight in World War I. He was wounded twice, then in 1916, returned to Canada and was medically discharged. One year later, he recovered and joined the Royal Flying Corp. He became a commissioned pilot, served as a flight instructor in the United Kingdom, and then returned to Canada in 1928 to work as a pilot with Western Canada Airways Limited. He did air mail deliveries across the prairies, performed search and rescue in the Arctic, and did one of the first mapping flights of the Antarctic. It made him just one of a few pilots to fly at the north and south poles. Over his career, Hollick-Kenyon flew forty-five aircraft types, amassing 14,000 flight hours. He was inducted as a Member of Canada's Aviation Hall of Fame in 1974.

Hotel Grand/Hagmann Block

98 Street and 107 Avenue

This four-storey structure was built in 1913 at this location because it was the city's bustling financial, business, and residential district.

It was constructed as an investment property by a Local farmer, John Hagmann. It was to help the thousands of people arriving in Edmonton during the first economic boom. Hagmann lost the building to creditors when the economy went bust during the First World War. But in 1927, it opened again and was operated as a convent for the next 45 years until it closed in 1972. It sat empty for many years, then in 2006, the city gave this place its municipal historic designation. In 2011, it was converted to small one-bedroom apartments for low-income earners.

John Hagmann did well with his farm. Today, the area north of the Yellowhead Trail, between 121 Street and St. Albert Trail, where his farm used to be, is now known as The Haggman Estate Industrial Area.

Hotel Macdonald

100 Street and 100 Avenue

It was a grand vision built for the Grand Trunk Pacific Railway. The original ten-storey hotel, a marvel of its time, boasted one hundred and seventy-five rooms. As construction commenced in September 1912, the estimated cost was $1.25 million. However, the grandeur of the project was such that the actual cost soared to just under $2.5 million. The interior alone cost $750,000. The hotel was to be unveiled in all its splendour in time for the first train arriving in Edmonton on July 6, 1915.

Over the years, Hotel Macdonald has proudly hosted many visitors, including political leaders, rock stars, and Royalty. However, the Royal visit of King George IV and the Queen Mother in 1939 stands out as one of the most significant events in the hotel's history, a moment that reverberates through time.

With a need for additional hotel space, A sixteen-storey addition opened in 1953, adding three hundred more rooms. That portion was demolished in 1986. There were plans to tear down the entire hotel as it fell into disrepair. In 1985, the building received a municipal heritage designation from the city.

Canadian Pacific Hotels bought the hotel in 1988, preserving its splendour. A three-year renovation project brought the building back to its former glory, and a $20-million refurbishment was injected.

The 'Mac' remains not just a hotel but a symbol of the city's rich history and grandeur. Standing tall as one of the city's best-known landmarks.

Hudson's Bay Company Building

Jasper Avenue and 103 Street

The HBC Building dates back to 1893 on this site. This structure was built in stages, the first in 1938, for one million dollars. Over 20,000 people would rush through the doors of the building on opening day, November 14th, 1939. A third-floor addition happened in 1949 for $500,000. Another expansion was announced in 1954, costing 3.2 million dollars, doubling the building size and making it one of the largest department stores in the country. Business boomed for several decades, but HBC moved to Edmonton Centre in 1995 as the retail landscape changed. After occupying this location for over 100 years, they closed this store altogether.

The University of Alberta needed space, so they purchased the building and opened it to students in September 2007, renaming it "Enterprise Square." In 1989, the building received its historic designation.

Hull Block

97 Street and 106 Avenue

It was built by William Hull, who came to Canada with his brother John in 1873. They were involved in several businesses, including construction and the cattle industry in Edmonton and Calgary. They built the Hull Block in early 1914 for $35,000; it was designed for small retail businesses on the main floor and apartments above with high-end finishes to create a place rich with character, comfort and class. It was the largest building in the area.

Thomson Drugs was one of the earliest tenants of The Hull Block, a tenant who had worked on the premises for several decades.

Despite its historical significance, The Hull Block, like many pre-World War I buildings, fell victim to neglect. Over the years, the landlord's lack of maintenance led to its gradual deterioration, threatening to erase its rich history.

The 1990s saw a resurgence in this part of town, breathing new life into The Hull Block. In 2001, the city recognized its historical value and granted it a historic designation. This paved the way for its revitalization, as it was purchased by a prominent Alberta anthropologist with a vision. An architect specializing in the conservation of historical buildings was brought in, ensuring no corners were cut in the meticulous restoration of the exterior and interior finishes. The renovations were completed in 2005, marking a new chapter in the history of The Hull Block.

Immigration Hall

100 Street and 105 Avenue

This two-storey structure with a full basement was built by the federal Department of Public Works during the Great Depression in 1930. It provided free short-term accommodation for the influx of new immigrants and settlers. The location was chosen to be near the former Canadian National main railway station. This place was quite busy for a couple of decades, especially with the discovery of oil near Leduc, which triggered another wave of immigration to Alberta.

After serving as an Immigration Hall until 1951, this building transitioned to house offices for the Department of Immigration and Citizenship Court until 1969, showcasing its adaptability and historical significance.

Many immigration Halls were constructed after World War I over fifty years, but just three are still standing in western Canada. Today, this building is operated by the Hope Mission. It received its Municipal Historic designation this week in 2009.

Imperial Bank of Canada Building

Jasper Avenue and 100 Street

The Imperial Bank of Canada was the first chartered bank in the city. They opened in Edmonton in 1891, two blocks west of this intersection. A new place was needed, so a branch was constructed on this site in 1908. When that one became too small, this seven-storey structure opened in 1954. On June 1, 1961, the largest merger of two chartered banks in Canadian history happened when The Canadian Bank of Commerce and The Imperial Bank of Canada merged to form the Canadian Imperial Bank of Commerce or as we know it today as, CIBC.

The bank operated out of this location until 2000. In 2003, the Edmonton Chamber of Commerce purchased it. It was renovated and renamed the World Trade Center Edmonton. This place received its municipal historic designation in 2004.

International Harvester Company

109 Street and 104 Avenue

This building was constructed for the International Harvester Company, a manufacturing company that started on July 28, 1902. They became the world's largest truck, tractor, and farm equipment company. In the late 1970s, Canadian sales reached over $1 billion. The company even offered a tractor school to teach you how to operate their equipment. This place was built in 1913 for its showroom, warehouse, and offices.

The International Harvester Company was one of the city's largest employers. They operated out of there until the 1950s. The property was later purchased and renamed by the Dorchester Investment Company.

One hundred years later, this historic warehouse is a boutique office space with loft ceilings and the original brick and beam interior.

Iron Works Building

96 Street and 104 Avenue

Built in 1909 by James and Thomas Cornwall, this place was essential to the construction boom, as they manufactured iron, steel and brass. The city's population in 1909 was 23,000; ten years later, that grew to 60,000. The brothers sold the building in 1927, and it continued to be used for manufacturing products such as boilers and plows. This place has fallen into disrepair in the last few decades, and the owner applied for a demolition permit. The city recognized the property's value and acquired it in 2016 to preserve it. A twenty-one million dollar renovation took place, with completion scheduled in late 2024.

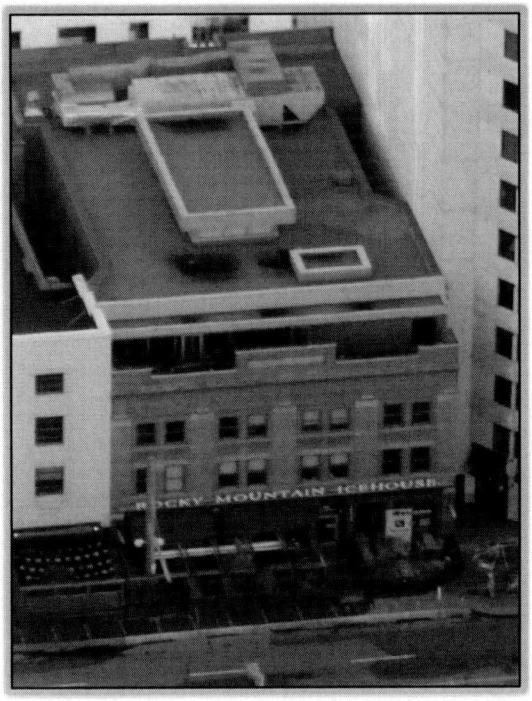

Jasper Block

Jasper Avenue and 105 Street

Built in 1909 for $30,000, this building was the first constructed west of 105 Street, marking downtown expansion to the west. The upper floors were apartments, while the ground floor housed commercial businesses such as a retail hat store, ladies' clothing, and insurance.

John Kelly had a hand in building this; he was one of Edmonton's early successful businessmen. Starting as a blacksmith in 1902, he did real estate and then developed commercial buildings, of which a few remain. This place received its Municipal Historic designation in 2004.

Jasper House Hotel

Jasper Avenue by 97 Street

James Goodridge began laying the bricks here in June 1882 and opened the hotel in August.

This was the first fully brick-built building between Winnipeg and Vancouver. Goodridge used it to his advantage in his advertising.

It remained Edmonton's only all-brick structure for nine years. New owners came and went over the decades, and with each one, new renovations happened. This hotel was added on several times, first in 1884, then in 1907, 1910, 1940, 1950, and 1958.

At one point, Jasper House started to collapse. A cracking noise was heard on the north side, and the building slowly started to fall. Heavy rain one night was to blame. They were able to stabilize the structure until it was properly fixed.

While not currently under threat of demolition, this 140-plus-year-old hotel is worth watching. After being neglected for about fifty years, repairs are finally taking place. Hopefully, with redevelopment, it will survive.

Jasper Place High School

163 Street and 89 Avenue

1961 marked the opening of Jasper Place High School, a significant event that drew a crowd of one thousand people, including the Royal Canadian Air Force. This was the largest school between Vancouver and Winnipeg, a title it held even before the expansions in 1962 and 1969. In 1962, the school almost closed its doors due to a heavy rain storm. This area was all dirt, including the roads that soaked up the water and came close to filling the main floor with mud.

In 1964, the Town of West Jasper Place, with a population of 38,000, merged with the City of Edmonton. The students didn't want this to happen, so they rebelled against the school district. To this day, those students are still recognized, as the school's sports teams are called the "Rebels." Those 'rebel' students also walked out of class in 1969 because the school didn't have a smoking room.

Many well-known people have attended J.P., including country singer/producer Adam Gregory, NHL goalie and broadcaster Kelly Hrudey, and Oilers owner Darryl Katz.

Jasper Place High School is still consistently recognized as one of Canada's top-performing high schools. It is the proud host of the REB Invitational Basketball tournament, a prestigious event that draws teams across North America. The school also organizes a 24-hour bike-a-thon, with all proceeds supporting the Make-a-Wish Foundation.

J.B. Little Brickyard House

90 Street and 100 Avenue

James Brown Little moved here in 1892 after learning brickwork down east. He purchased ten acres of land in the Riverdale neighbourhood, specifically for the natural clay to make the bricks. The kiln fired one year later, and as business was booming, he purchased an additional twenty acres.

The company employed many Edmontonians who moved to the area, including the Littles, as they built this house in 1905. If any structure in Edmonton was made from bricks in the early 1900s, it likely came from this factory. By the mid-1930s, they would be producing about 35,000 bricks per day. The company operated for ninety-eight years until 1990.

The Little family lived here until 2000. In 2015, it was converted into a cafe called "The Little Brick," keeping the history alive. The house was designated a municipal historic site in 2017.

JJ Duggan's House

Saskatchewan Drive and 105 Street

John Joseph Duggan moved to Strathcona in 1891 and started a lumber business. He also sold agricultural equipment, invested in real estate, became an alderman in 1899, and was twice elected Mayor of Strathcona. He built this house in 1907, overlooking the North Saskatchewan River Valley in the style of many upper-middle-class houses at the time. It has two fireplaces, a veranda, and a second-story balcony.

Duggan lived here for twenty-four years; in 1940, this house was converted into a duplex and eventually bought by the city. It was slated for demolition to make way for a road. Thankfully, the project didn't happen, and this place was spared. The house fell into disrepair but was saved in 1981 when the Architects Association of Alberta bought it. They have used it as their main office ever since. Duggan has a neighbourhood named after him, down by the Whitemud and 111 Street. The province deemed this structure a historic resource in 1982 and the city in 2013.

John A. McDougall School

107 Street and 109 Avenue

It opened in 1913 for $160,000. This story is more about the man than the building. This school is named after a predominate Edmontonian. McDougall moved here in 1877, and he was a businessman. He owned a general store, was a fur trader, one of the founders of St. John Ambulance in Alberta, an alderman, an MLA, and the city's fourth mayor. McDougall played a significant role in getting the automatic telephone system in the city and the Low Level Bridge built. If that's not enough, he also worked in real estate. He established a financial and mortgage corporation that is still in business today and is considered one of the oldest businesses in the province. A legacy worth having a school named after. Over a century later, the school still operates for kindergarten to grade six students.

John Walter Houses

At the bottom of Walterdale Hill

The first house was built in 1875, just a few years after Walter's arrived in the Edmonton area. It was the first residence on the south bank of the river. Also, used as an office for his cable ferry, freight service, and telegraph station. When it became too small, he built his second house in 1884.

He kept growing his business empire, which included a general store, lumber mill, blacksmith operation, and coal mine. This all helped him become the city's first millionaire in 1901, so he needed a bigger house, and that's when the third was constructed. It was one of the larger homes in Edmonton and one of the first to have electricity.

John died in 1920, and his wife continued to live here until she passed away in 1942. In 1959, the houses were moved closer together to create a museum to preserve the memory of one of the city's pioneers.

Jubilee Auditorium

87 Avenue and 114 Street

To celebrate Alberta's 50th anniversary, construction of the Northern Alberta Jubilee Auditorium commenced in the summer of 1955 and took two years to complete. There is a seating capacity of approximately twenty-five hundred, it is a versatile venue, hosting a variety of performances, from concerts to comedians and even graduations. Since 1966, it has been the proud home of the Alberta Ballet and hosts the Edmonton Opera and the Ukrainian Shumka Dancers.

Extensive renovations were undertaken in 2005 as part of the Province's Centennial to modernize and restore the Jubilee. In 2009, the Jubilee Auditorium, or more commonly called 'The Jub,' was the busiest theatre in Canada, selling over 146,000 tickets.

Kathleen Andrews Transit Garage

Fort Road by Yellowhead Trail

This facility was built to replace the Westwood Garage by NAIT. It was named after the first female bus driver in the city; she started in 1975. The 50,000 square metre facility was delayed in opening due to the strengthening of the cement floor to support the heavier weight of the electric buses. Since its completion in 2021, the garage has been home to three hundred buses, thirty-five maintenance bays and eight hundred staff. The exterior of the building has latitude coordinates of other regions around the world that are the same as Edmonton.

Kelly/Ramsey Building

100 A Street and 101 Avenue

John Kelly started his career as a blacksmith before he became a real estate developer. Kelly built this darker brick structure (on the right) in 1914.

James Ramsey was known as Edmonton's "Merchant Prince." In 1911, he opened a successful retail store. On the first day of business, Ramsey did seventy-five hundred dollars in sales. Needing more space, he expanded into the Kelly Building before constructing his place (lighter brick building on the left) in 1927 for $150,000. A year later, Ramsey decided to retire, and he sold his business, but not the building, to Eaton's for one million dollars. The buildings changed hands several times over the decades, becoming home to government offices, retail stores, apartments and restaurants. In 2009, both structures were severely damaged by fire.

In 2011, the bricks were removed, cleaned, and re-installed within a couple of feet of their original location to honour the past. To create something new, a twenty-eight-storey structure was constructed on top of the Kelly/Ramsey Building, with a new name: Enbridge Centre.

King Edward School

101 Street and 85 Avenue

The school was built in 1913 for $180,000. Like many other schools around the city at that time, the outside was constructed with red bricks. When you enter, there is a fifteen-foot ceiling, wide hallways, oak mouldings, panelled walls, and marble stairs.

Initially, there were seventeen classrooms, and this was the first city school to have a large assembly hall on the ground floor instead of the top floor. That was for easy access from the surrounding community. In 1939, the school was honoured with a visit from King George VI and Queen Elizabeth.

In 1992, it was renamed The Academy at King Edward. The school across the street, built in 1959, kept the King Edward name for kindergarten through grade six students.

Kingston Powell Building

97 Street and 102 Avenue

This structure was built in 1907 and named after its owner, Kingston Powell. He was one of the first farmers in the area, dating back to the 1880s. Powell constructed this building as an investment property, taking advantage of the boom before the First World War.

At the turn of the century, many buildings, including this one, had stores on the ground level and residential spaces above, and typically, signage was painted on the outside along the top. Powell eventually lost some of his investments and returned to his farm in the Calder area.

Today, this place is a law office, and the structure received its municipal historic designation in 2002.

Knox Church

104 Street and 84 Avenue

This church has had a few name changes over the years. When it opened in 1907, it was known as Knox Presbyterian Church, then Knox United Church and now home to Knox Evangelical Free Church.

More than just a building, it was a community hub, a place of gathering and growth. It was built for $165,000 and was a significant event when it opened. Alberta's first premier, Alexander Rutherford, and William Griesbach, the mayor of Edmonton, were among the esteemed guests. As funds were raised, the church expanded, adding a pipe organ in 1911, a new hall, a gymnasium, kitchen, and social room in 1950, and stained glass in 1957.

The church remains one of the oldest in Edmonton; it received its Provincial Historic designation in 1976 and by the city in 2013.

Koermann Block

96 Street and 102A Avenue

This building is in the oldest part of Edmonton's first commercial district. Gustave Koermann built it in 1911. It housed a German-language newspaper, commercial tenants, and residential units on the second floor. The paper did quite well until World War I broke out. Then was classified as an enemy, and all its assets were seized.

1919, the Ukrainian Bookstore moved in for six years before relocating in 1925. The building then had a large variety of businesses in between being vacant for many years.

The building is currently empty and on the historic list, awaiting its designation.

Lambton Block

97 Street and 110A Avenue

In 1914, John Robert Boyle paid $25,000 to have this building constructed. Boyle named the block after Lambton County in Ontario, where he was from. He became a member of the Alberta Legislative Assembly and was appointed to the Supreme Court of Alberta in 1924. The Boyle community in Edmonton and the Alberta town of Boyle were named in his honour.

The Lambton Block has six sides to accommodate the odd-shaped corner lot. The three-storey building originally had twenty-two apartments and stores at street level. Being so close to the Royal Alexandra Hospital, in the 1920s the top floor became home for the nurses. The block included bachelor and one-bedroom suites; some apartments had fireplaces and bathrooms. In 1980, the main floor became a law office, but eventually, it changed to residential use only. The building received its municipal historic designation in 2003.

Land Titles Building

100 Avenue and 105 Street

This building was constructed in 1893 as the regional Land, Timber and Registry Office. When people moved to the west, this is where they would register their claim to crown land.

As the Edmonton area rapidly grew, a bigger building was needed. So, the federal government tried to move to a new location in the town of Strathcona, but Edmonton residents engaged in an armed standoff with the North West Mounted Police.

In 1912, land titles finally moved out. Before the First World War, this became the Victoria Armouries. Over the next few decades, the Armoury was home to a series of Edmonton regiments.

In 1949, the Alberta Department of Health took over the building, which eventually sat empty for several years before being renovated.

This is Alberta's oldest federal administration building. It was declared a provincial historic structure in 1977.

Latta Bridge

Jasper Avenue and 92 Street

The bridge is named after David Latta, an early influence in the city as a blacksmith, Northwest Mounted Police Constable, and city alderman. He constructed the first bridge in 1911. It wasn't pretty, but it did the job for two decades for the odd horse, cart, and streetcar.

As traffic increased, the city condemned the bridge and tore it down in 1929. The Great Depression prevented the city from rebuilding until 1936. The cost was $25,000, and some leftover material from the renovations at the High Level Bridge was used.

When the bridge was completed, a dance party was held to celebrate. Over two thousand people showed up the night before it opened. That bridge stood for eighty-six years until 2022, when it was demolished. The third version of the Latta Bridge took fourteen months to construct and cost $21.2 million. Hopefully, this bridge will last at least another eighty-six years.

A bronze historical marker was placed on this bridge in 1936. It was Edmonton's third-ever historical marker.

Legislature Annex Building

97 Avenue and 107 Street

The Annex structure was built for the Alberta Government Telephones headquarters, AGT.

Construction commenced in 1951 and took two years to take shape. Initially a six-storey structure, it expanded to twelve floors in 1964, reflecting the city and province's growth. This transformation made it one of the city's tallest buildings. Interestingly, upon completion, some dubbed it an 'eyesore' and a 'Green Monster.'

Again, as growth continued, this space became too small. AGT moved out in 1971. The province took over the building, which housed various government, Members of the Legislative Assembly, and Official Opposition party offices.

Over the years, it fell into disrepair, and the cost to fix it is over half the building's value. Demolition started in the spring of 2022 and took about six months. The site is now green space.

LeMarchand Mansion

100 Avenue and 115 Street

René Le Marchand was active in real estate, an investor, and a member of the Edmonton Chamber of Commerce after arriving in Edmonton from Paris in 1905. He started construction on this building in 1909, a forty-three-suite apartment block overlooking the river valley.

The LeMarchand Mansion, an H-shaped building, boasts a red brick facade with intricate sandstone window details. In its time, it was a symbol of modernity. Each suite was equipped with a gas-burning stove, a dumb waiter, and at least one fireplace, a luxury ahead of its time. However, such luxury came at a cost, with the rent for the suites reaching up to one hundred dollars a month, a significant amount in those days.

Bryan Hall, a well-known sports reporter lived here for many years before the former apartment building was converted to office space and declared a historic structure in 1977.

Louise McKinney Park

Grierson Hill and 99 Street

Some of Edmonton's lush green spaces were once dumps. Edmonton's first dump was located on the north bank of the river at this location.

People began using the site as early as 1894. By 1912, the first of several petitions were filed to shut it down due to the smell, the danger to public health, and the number of fires.

Not only was it the dump, but the City used the garbage to stabilize the river bank. Kids played down here, and during the Great Depression, people lived here! Homes were built from whatever could be found. There was no electricity, running water or natural gas. Despite these challenges, the community thrived. As time passed, homes were actually bought and sold. Most homes were single rooms and filled with furniture that was either found or made.

The City formally acknowledged the community in 1932, but when typhoid fever was discovered, the City issued eviction notices in 1938. Everyone had one month to vacate. When the community was cleared, the homes were destroyed, and today, from this once challenging site, a beautiful park has emerged.

Low Level Bridge

Rossdale Road

Completed in 1900, this was the first bridge across the North Saskatchewan River in the city. Originally called the Edmonton Bridge, it was renamed the Low Level after the High Level Bridge opened in 1913.

The design was to carry trains before street cars used it. As traffic volume increased, a second bridge was built in 1949. One span was for trains, and the other was for two-way vehicle traffic.

In 1915, the Great Flood happened. The river rose forty-two feet in less than forty-eight hours, bringing the water level to the bridge deck. With all the debris in the river pushing against it, there was a fear the bridge would get washed away. In hopes it wouldn't, trains were parked on each end of the bridge to weigh it down. It worked, and the water level went down almost as fast as it went up. Over a century later, over 40,000 vehicles use the bridge daily.

Light Rail Transit

Construction commenced in 1974 for sixty-five million dollars. April 23, 1978, saw the grand opening of the LRT system, four months before the Commonwealth Games opened. The line had five stations along the Canadian National rail line from Belvedere to the Coliseum, to Commonwealth Stadium, then to the Churchill and Central Stations downtown. Edmonton was the first city in Western Canada to operate a rapid transit system and the first city in North America with a population under one million to have one as well. In 1981, a 2.2-kilometre extension was added north to Clareview for ten million dollars. 1983 brought two more stations online downtown, another one in 1989 before it crossed the river in 1992.

Currently, there are twenty-nine stations over three lines. The metro line has the most stations, with fifteen, and the deepest one in the system is at the university, twenty-three metres below the surface.

M.E. LaZerte High School

144 Avenue and 66 Street

Built when the northeast part of the city was just about to boom, this school opened in 1969, costing just under $4.4 million. There are three buildings that make up the school, all were constructed at the same time. The main one has classrooms, another has two gymnasiums, and the third has a vocational area. This school was designed with no windows in all the classrooms. That was to help keep students focused so they didn't get distracted.

It is named after Milton Ezra LaZerte, who dedicated his life to education. He worked at the University of Alberta in 1925 and became the Dean of the Faculty of Education. He was also the president of the Alberta Teachers' Association, the Canadian Teachers' Federation, and the Canadian Education Association. He also served on the Canada and United States Committee on Education. The school is still going strong, home to 2,200 students.

MacCosham Warehouse

109 Street and 103 Avenue

Roderick Vic MacCosham headed to Edmonton in 1906 from Bryson, Quebec. He worked in various industries before he settled into the storage business. He inherited $20,000, bought this warehouse in 1913, and started the MacCosham Storage & Distributing Company. Two years later, he received a contract to haul and store goods for the railroad. He did it with a horse and wagon before changing to motorized vehicles. Over the years and merging with other companies, MacCosham doubled in size to become one of the largest distribution networks in North America. All with the simple start of storing products in this warehouse.

Outgrowing this structure, they moved out. The building was used for other businesses and sat empty for a while before being turned into loft apartments. The outside has been modernized, but the interior has many original wood beams and posts. Over a century later, the company is still going strong and is operating in the railroad industry.

MacEwan University

104 Avenue from 105 - 112 Streets

This facility opened its doors on November 6, 1993. It is named after Dr. Grant MacEwan, a professor, historian, mayor, author, and the Lieutenant Governor of Alberta.

The university started as a community college in 1971. One campus was in the Old Scona School building, and the other was in a commercial building on 118 Avenue and 80 Street. As enrollment grew, so did the number of campuses, including one in Millwoods, downtown and another in the west end. To better serve the students, consolidations of the programs moved to downtown.

In 2012, Grant MacEwan Community College became a University, and a year later, the name changed to MacEwan University.

From its modest beginnings, MacEwan had an enrollment of four hundred students; today, there are over 18,300.

MacLean Block

107 Street and Jasper Avenue

Constructed in 1909 for Doctor James MacLean, it was the westernmost commercial building in Edmonton at the time.

The three-storey building cost $35,000 to construct and was designed with retail stores at the ground level, including the Imperial Bank of Canada in the 1920s, offices on the second floor, and rooming apartments on the third.

Over the years, the MacLean Block changed hands several times, each transition leaving its mark on the building's identity. By the mid-1970s, the building's condition had deteriorated considerably, with the rooming house conditions considered barely livable.

In 1977, renovations were completed on the outside. The interior was gutted and rebuilt to house modern commercial and office spaces. Today, Audrey's Book Store occupies the main floor. In 1983, it received its historical designation.

Magrath Mansion

Ada Boulevard and 62 Street

William Magrath came to Edmonton in 1904. He was a businessman and a real estate developer. In 1912, he built an upscale house on five city lots overlooking the river valley.

This three-storey home has fourteen rooms, an indoor pool in the basement, a central control panel for all the lights, an intercom system, a telephone connection in every room, a built-in vacuum and a burglar alarm.

After William's passing in 1920, the mansion's ownership saw several changes. When his wife was unable to pay the property taxes, the sheriff seized the house in 1931. In turn, the city bought it a couple of years later. The mansion sat empty until 1937 when it was rented as suites. It was returned as a private home until 2021, then gifted to Concordia University. This place received its provincial historic designation in 1975.

Malone Block

104 Street and 81 Avenue

This building is named after Thomas Malone, who moved to Edmonton in 1905 and bought a mercantile business. He constructed this building in 1908, and it became one of the leading department stores in the city. Wanting to be more busy, Thomas served as president of the South Side Community League and the Federation of Community Leagues. In 1919, he became a Catholic School Board member and sat on the city council until 1923.

Many have walked or driven by this small century-plus-old building, perhaps without fully appreciating its rich history. Like many other buildings in the Old Strathcona area, the Malone Block has changed owners and housed dozens of businesses that have opened and closed. It is a mystery waiting to be unravelled, a story waiting to be told, and it would be fascinating to crack the code and have a conversation with the walls as these structures continue to stand the test of time.

Massey Ferguson Building

106 Street and 103 Avenue

Originally constructed in 1947 as a showroom for tractor sales, this versatile building saw a significant transition in the early 1970s. The Healy Family, owners of an established Ford car dealership, purchased the property to expand their business. The showroom was transformed into a Ford dealership, a role it served until 2011. When the dealership moved to Sherwood Park, the building was closed.

In 2015, a proposal to build three-forty-storey condo towers incorporating this historic building was made, offering a promising vision for the future of this iconic structure. Although the sunset clause expired in 2022, leaving the place vacant, the potential for redevelopment still holds hope for the building's future.

Matt Berry Neighbourhood

66 Street and 153 Avenue

This area is named in honour of Arthur Massey 'Matt' Berry. Born in 1888 near Ottawa, Berry served with the 30th Wellington Rifles as a captain in the First World War before transferring to the Royal Flying Corps. He graduated as a pilot and as a flying instructor. After the war, Berry flew a lot in the north, including Alberta, and out to the Hudson Bay area. He was the first pilot to land at Baker Lake Northwest Territories and the first to complete a same-day return flight of sixteen hundred kilometres, between Great Bear Lake and Edmonton.

Berry was involved in several dramatic and difficult rescues in the mid-1930s, finding missing pilots and bringing them safely home. On one of the missions, he discovered two men who had been missing for thirty days. It was one of the largest and most publicized searchers in Canadian history. He served in World War II and continued to fly into the 1950s before getting involved in some mining ventures. He passed away on May 12, 1970, and was posthumously inducted into Canada's Aviation Hall of Fame in 1974.

Mayfield Neighbourhood

107 to 111 Avenues and 156 Street to Mayfield Road

This area is named after a well-known Edmonton pilot and probably the best known Wilfred Reid May, a.k.a. Wop May. In 1916, he enlisted and became a Sergeant Gunner before being transferred to the Royal Flying Corps. He received his wings, and with only 55 hours of flying time, May was posted in France as a fighter pilot. In 1918, he was involved in an aerial dogfight with the Red Baron, a German fighter pilot ace. As May was being chased, his fellow pilot and friend, Roy Brown, shot the Red Baron down! After the war, he returned and started May Airplane Limited, the first air service in Edmonton.

In January 1929, May and his co-pilot, Vic Horner, embarked on a daring mercy flight in an open cockpit aircraft from Edmonton to Fort Vermilion, a journey of nearly one thousand kilometres in -33°C to deliver life-saving medication. His contributions to the aviation industry were not limited to commercial ventures. He founded Canadian Pacific Airlines and established airbases in the north and across the prairies. During World War II, he trained pilots and pioneered the concept of aerial rescue crews, saving the lives of numerous airmen. May's unwavering dedication to aviation earned him numerous awards from various countries, including the Medal of Freedom from the United States and the title of "Officer of the Order of the British Empire."

In Canada, he was inducted as a Member of Canada's Aviation Hall of Fame. He was awarded the Trans-Canada Trophy for his flying achievements and the Distinguished Flying Cross. Stompin' Tom Connors even wrote a song about him. May is declared a National Historic Person, including being on the list of the "One Hundred Citizens of the Century." He has a neighbourhood named after him, along with a lake, river, many aircraft, and a rock on Mars! Wop May accomplished all this and more in a short life of just fifty-six years.

McCauley School

95 Street and 107 Avenue

It was built in 1911, but the official opening happened on March 7, 1912. This twelve-room school cost $93,800. The school was named after Matthew McCauley, the first Mayor of Edmonton and a Member of the Legislative Assembly in the first Alberta Legislature. Among the building's features are the science rooms in the basement, a large library on the second floor, and an assembly hall on the third. The assembly hall also served as the gymnasium until the new gym was constructed in 1961.

When it closed in 2010, the school served the neighbourhood for almost a century. The Edmonton Intercultural Centre now occupies these walls.

McConachie Neighbourhood

66 Street and 167 Avenue

George William Grant McConachie was born in 1909. He attended the University of Alberta but left during his first year with the attraction to take up flying. McConachie received his licence at age twenty, bought an aircraft one year later, and flew to the north to transport fish. As with many other bush pilots, he performed emergency flights, which resulted in the saving of lives.

In 1933, he founded United Air Transport Company, which had scheduled flights to Whitehorse. McConachie also contributed to forming other airlines. One of them was Canadian Pacific, as he was named President in 1947. He was instrumental in flying to faraway lands such as Tokyo, Peru, Portugal, Spain, and many other destinations. He also discovered air paths over polar regions are the shortest and most economical ways to fly. His most spectacular venture was the great circle route over the Arctic Ocean, non-stop from Vancouver to Amsterdam. He became a member of Canada's Aviation Hall of Fame in 1974.

McDougall United Church

101 Street and 100 Avenue

This site has seen three churches constructed on it. The original was built of logs in 1873, the second was a wood frame church constructed in 1892, and the third one was built of bricks in 1909.

The current structure cost $85,000 to build and could seat up to twenty-five hundred people, a tenth of the city's population at the time.

During both World Wars, the church was an important place. It was used as a centre to send thousands of packages to soldiers and a collection centre for the Red Cross. In 1920, this was the first home of the Edmonton Symphony and the original home of the Edmonton Opera in 1963. This building did receive its historic designation in 2015.

The first version of the McDougall United Church was one of the first buildings built outside the walls of Fort Edmonton. It still exists, having been moved to the current Fort Edmonton Park to serve as a museum.

McIntyre Park

83 Avenue and 104 Street

Dr. Wilbert McIntyre was born in 1867 in Ontario. He first travelled west in 1891 and returned to stay in 1902. McIntyre was a respected doctor who wanted to be involved in the community. He supported building the High Level Bridge connecting Strathcona with Edmonton. He was elected a Member of Parliament in 1906. That made him the first elected representative in the new Province of Alberta. His constituency was huge, extending east to Lloydminster and south to Innisfail.

Dr. McIntyre's sudden death in 1909, when he was forty-two years old, it was a profound loss for the community. His funeral, one of the largest at that time in northern Alberta, was a testament to his popularity and the impact he had on the people.

In his honour, a commemorative fountain was built in 1913, a symbol of Dr. McIntyre's legacy, and stood two blocks south of this location on 81 Avenue for thirty-nine years. It was tragically destroyed in 1952 after a car hit it. The community's respect for Dr. McIntyre's memory was evident in the meticulous recreation of the fountain. The current fountain, a replica of the original, was unveiled in 1991, just three years after this area was renamed Dr. Wilbert McIntyre Park.

McBain Camera Store

Mayfield Road and 104 Avenue

This store is named after Ross McBain, who was born in 1924. McBain joined the military and served in World War II because he thought he would be "missing all the action." He had lots of training, mainly in a Harvard and a Corsair airplane, but saw little action. That's because on the day of his first operational flight, the United States dropped the atomic bomb, and the war was over a few days later. When McBain returned to Canada, he took a photography course and decided to enter the photo business. He opened his first camera store in the city on August 10, 1949.

He was the first to video Edmonton Eskimo football games at the request of the coaching staff. They wanted to see which players were making mistakes. McBain had many accomplishments, including working with Northlands, the Edmonton Chamber of Commerce, and the Alberta Aviation Council. He was the founding president of the Better Business Bureau and the Director of the Edmonton Eskimos.

Ross McBain passed away in 2018 at the age of 94.

McKay Avenue School

99 Avenue and 104 Street

Edmonton's first schoolhouse was built in 1881 for an estimated cost of $968. The glass windows were shipped from Ontario. They were put into barrels of molasses to keep the panes from breaking. There is a story that the kids were invited down to Fort Edmonton when the glass arrived, and they licked the glass clean! Not only was the field trip educational, it was nutritional! The first class for Edmonton Public had 28 students. By 1888, enrollment had grown to 82, and an addition was added to the school and built for $1,550.

In 1890, a night school program was introduced, three nights a week, to cater to students who could not attend classes in the day. The schoolhouse stayed open until 1905 when McKay Avenue School was built for $44,000. The school was named after Dr. William MacKay, a Hudson's Bay Company officer and surgeon. McKay Avenue is the oldest school still standing in the city. The school's third-floor assembly hall was used during the first two sessions of the Alberta Legislature in 1906 and 1907.

McKay Avenue remained an operating school until 1983. Today, Edmonton Public Schools use the building for their Archives and Museum. The district now consists of more than two hundred and ten schools, with over 10,500 staff and over 120,000 students. This school was designated a provincial historical building in 1976.

McKenney Building

104 Street and 101 Avenue

Henry McKenney moved throughout Canada and the United States before coming west from Manitoba. He settled in St. Albert in 1883 and started his first business. He was involved in the fur trade, became a postmaster and operated a mill, among other interests. McKenny was elected as a member of the Alberta Legislature three consecutive times, starting in 1905. He purchased this property in 1903 as an investment but did not construct the namesake building until 1912, costing $40,000. The building housed a footwear store, a supply company and a market. McKenny died in 1921, and the building was sold. As time passed, the building deteriorated. It underwent renovations in 1979. After being modernized and saving the interior brickwork, this building is available for lease. It is on the city's historic list for preservation.

McLeod Building

100 Street and 101 Avenue

It was named after Kenneth McLeod, one of Edmonton's pioneers, arriving in the city in 1881. He became an alderman, a public school trustee, a construction contractor, and a real estate speculator. He wanted to build Edmonton's most remarkable commercial structure with his name on it. Completed in 1915, this nine-storey building was the tallest on the skyline for thirty-six years, until 1951. It was the first building in the city to be wired with conduit. The interior had the finest wood and marble. The $600,000 building was over-constructed, using twelve hundred tons of steel. The footings are eleven square feet, large enough to support a fifty-storey building.

One of the early tenants was Alberta's first Premier, Alexander Rutherford's law firm. The former office building has eighty-eight condo units with retail space on the first floor. The province and the city gave the building its historic designation in 1995 and 2001.

McLeod Elementary School

59 Street and 148 Avenue

The school was built in 1972 for $492,000. The neighbourhood and the school were named after Murdoch McLeod, an early pioneer with the Hudson Bay Company in 1861. He moved to Fort Edmonton in 1879 with others after escaping prison from the Louis Riel Rebellion, where he was to be executed. Here, he started the first school in the fort and later farmed land in the northeast part of the city. When this school had the official opening, Murdoch's grandchildren and great-grandchildren attended. This school is home to approximately four hundred students from kindergarten to grade six. The school celebrated its 50th anniversary in 2022.

Mercer Building

104 Avenue and 104 Street

In 1911, John B. Mercer, a key player in the liquor and cigar trade, constructed the Mercer Building. This warehouse, designed to accommodate his growing business, also served as a cold storage facility for The Calgary Brewing Company. Its four floors and advanced design made it a pioneer in its field, and it was considered one of Alberta's most modern and complete cold storage plants.

It was strategically built close to the railway to transport his products, a location crucial for the efficient operation of his business. Originally, this structure had four floors; a fire destroyed the top two floors in 1922. When it was rebuilt, loading bay doors were added, and it only had three storeys.

After almost eighty years, the building started to fall into disrepair, but in 2010, it received a second life as the warehouse was rehabilitated. Inside, there is now a tavern, technology, start-ups, retail, and other businesses, each contributing to the vibrant life of this historical building.

Metals Limited Building

104 Street and 102 Avenue

The Metals Limited Company, a wholesaler of mine and mill products, steamfitters and plumbing supplies, built this three-storey structure in 1914 for $40,000.

This place was constructed as a warehouse, so the ceilings are high. The Metals Building was the first building on the west side of 104 Street. It stood alone there for years, as that was the furthest west the downtown went, and because of the start of the Second World War. The business did improve, so they added to this structure in 1927. Over the years, several companies have been located here. The whole complex was renovated in the 1970s. This place received its municipal historic designation in 2002, and another expansion happened when they added The Century Tower in 2005.

Mill Creek Trestle Bridge

76 Avenue by 92 Street

Mill Creek Ravine received its name from a flour mill established in 1878. This area was essential to industry, including the mill, meatpacking plants, and a railway. In 1899, the Edmonton, Yukon and Pacific Railway constructed forty-five kilometres of track, including the line that followed the Mill Creek Ravine up to the North Saskatchewan River. This Trestle Bridge was completed in 1902. It was part of the first rail connection between the Town of Strathcona and Edmonton. Train passenger service happened until 1928, then used to haul coal until 1954. That's when the line was closed and the tracks removed before being turned into green space. In the late 1970s, the bridge was transformed into a path for pedestrians and bicyclists, showing its adaptability.

Today, the Mill Creek Trestle Bridge is a powerful symbol of our heritage. It is one of five in the ravine that remains in use as part of the Edmonton River Valley Trail System. Its significance was officially recognized in 2004 when it received its municipal historic designation. In 2018, the bridge underwent renovations, with twenty-five percent of the original wood still in use. This ongoing effort to preserve our history and make it accessible to future generations is a testament to our community's commitment and pride, instilling a deep sense of connection to our local history among the residents of Edmonton.

Milner Building

104 Street and 100 Avenue

This twelve-storey building was constructed in 1957 for the Northwestern Utilities Company, Canada's largest natural gas distributor. Since they were the most prominent company, they wanted the tallest building in Edmonton. The company dates back to 1923 under a federal government charter for producing and distributing natural gas. The building was named after Horatio Milner, who was born in 1889. He was a World War One veteran before becoming a lawyer and a businessman with extensive involvement in the oil and gas industry. He was on the first council of Northwestern Utilities Board from the start. He did all that by the age of thirty-four. He retired in 1969, the same year he received the Companion of the Order of Canada. That is the highest level of the Order of Canada. It is limited to one hundred and eighty living Canadians at any given time.

Northwestern moved out of here, and the building sold a couple of times. With office vacancy rates increasing, it is now being converted into two hundred and twenty residential units with retail on the ground level.

Northern Alberta Institute of Technology

Princess Elizabeth Avenue and 106 Street

This school is known as NAIT. In 1959, the idea was proposed by the provincial government to build a new vocational school in Edmonton. The fourteen-and-a-half million dollar construction project began in January 1962. The first classes started on October 1 of the same year. It didn't take long for student enrollment to fill this place. They expanded several times, once in 1965 and again in 1971. When they ran out of space again, an expansion happened across the street in 2002, 2007 and most recently in 2016.

What started as a modest tech school, with the first class of twenty-nine electrical students, today has thirty-six hundred students in forty-three different programs.

North Edmonton School

128 Avenue and 69 Street

This two-storey school opened in 1911. It was located in the Village of North Edmonton before this area became part of the city.

Four years later, it had an enrollment of one hundred and fifty students. 1923 and 1955 saw additions made to accommodate the growing student population. This school has had its problems. The building was known for being very cold in the winter, as the heating system was unreliable. Never mind 'snow days'; this school often had to close for 'cold days' because it couldn't be heated. In 1917, cracks were found in the foundation walls due to poor grading of the land around the building, which caused the basement to flood repeatedly. That happened for many decades, even into the 1990s. Due to low enrollment, this school was closed in 2005. A major overhaul happened to fix the foundation.

Today, this structure continues to serve the community as Balwin Villa. It is to help people with brain injuries, mental illness and early-onset dementia.

North Edmonton Telephone Exchange Building

101 Street and 112 Avenue

Edmonton was the first to install automatic telephones in North America in 1908. With over one thousand new subscribers signed on to the telephone system within a few years, the city built this place in 1912 to meet the needs of the growing city. The Exchange was built with enough equipment to serve 2000 subscribers. By 1919, the Exchange was working at capacity with one telephone for every five citizens.

With the expansion of the north side of the city, the Exchange couldn't keep up, so it was closed in 1958. Two years later, the City of Edmonton Archives created a local museum here. Historical vehicles were stored in the basement. Artifacts and photos were displayed on the main floor. The Archives outgrew this place by 1977. It took fifteen years to move into the retrofitted Prince of Wales Armouries. The Glenrose Rehabilitation Hospital purchased this place in 1993. They redesigned it to become a research lab for new technology in spinal cord injuries. It was the same year that this building received its historic recognition.

Northlands Coliseum

Wayne Gretzky Drive and 118 Avenue

Built in 1974 for 17.3 million dollars, this was the new home of the Edmonton Oilers. This place was also known as Edmonton Coliseum, Skyreach Centre, and Rexall Place. It opened on November 10, 1974, and on November 30, the first concert featured headliner Stevie Wonder. Of course, many would refer to this place as the "House Gretzky Built"!

The Coliseum was primarily used for hockey but also hosted many other events, including the Commonwealth Games, the World Men's Curling Championship, the World Junior Hockey Championships, the Canadian Figure Skating Championships, the NHL Entry Draft, the Canada Cup, and seven Stanley Cup finals!

The Oilers' played their final game in this building on April 6, 2016, against the Vancouver Canucks. The Oilers won 6–2, and Leon Draisaitl scored the last NHL goal.

In 2014, the Coliseum was the second busiest arena in Canada, the fifth busiest in North America, and the twenty-third busiest arena in the world, proving that Northlands was Edmonton's destination for entertainment! The Coliseum all has been silenced since the downtown arena was built.

Northlands Exhibition Grounds

Wayne Gretzky Drive and 118 Avenue

The Northlands Organization was initially called "The Edmonton Agricultural Society". It was developed to showcase livestock, vegetables, grain, and other locally produced products. The first exhibition was held on the original Fort Edmonton site in 1879. In 1910, it moved to this location, which at the time was known as Kirkness Lake. A year later, on April 28, 1911, the first airplane flight in Edmonton took off from the Exhibition Grounds when a pilot named Hugh Robinson lifted his Curtiss biplane into the air! Northlands and this area have advanced from an agricultural society to constructing the Edmonton Gardens Livestock Building in 1913, to the largest exhibition facility in Canada, and became the original home of the Edmonton Oilers. This facility was used by the armed forces for training in both world wars before changing into an entertainment district, hosting the first rodeo in conjunction with the fair in 1950.

In 1962, the exhibition adopted a gold rush theme and changed its name to Klondike Days. The first legal Casino in Canada, the Klondike Days Casino, was established on this site in 1967. Success continued into the 2000s with agricultural exhibits, horse racing, the midway, concerts, and other entertainment.

Northlands Race Track

Borden Park Road

Horse racing started in the city down in the Rossdale Neighbourhood. The Northlands track was opened in 1900, making it older than the province. As popularity grew, so did this place, expanding the horse stables and the grandstands. Northlands had nine hundred indoor seats and twenty-one hundred in the outdoor grandstand. There were three dining areas on the second floor.

This race track was the home of the Canadian Derby for six decades, dating back to 1957, making it among the best racing tracks in North America. Not only for the facility but for the massive crowds it drew. In the 1970s and 80s, this was the place to be, as it was packed with cheering fans, holding races five or six days a week, and some days, over one million dollars of betting would happen. The city closed this place for residential redevelopment. Northlands Park hung up the saddle after one hundred and eighteen years of horse racing on January 31, 2019.

Northwest Industries Hangar

Bush Pilot Road and 121 Street

A great Edmonton pilot, Leigh Brintnell, built this hangar. His flying career started in 1917 when he joined the Royal Flying Corps. He received his Private Pilots Licence and then became an instructor for pilots in the First World War. After the war, Brintnell flew around Great Bear Lake, Northwest Territories, photographing the ground formations from the air. As a result of his photos, uranium was discovered. He is at least partly responsible for focusing the attention of government, oil, and mining companies on the north. He worked at a few aviation companies and owned some as well. He helped create Canadian Pacific Airlines in 1942 with other bush pilots, such as Wop May. Most pilots fixed their own planes or took a mechanic on their flights. Brintnell thought it would be easier if pilots had a central place to do repairs, so he formed Aircraft Repair Limited. When World War II started, he changed the name to Northwest Industries and repaired warplanes. He started with 24 employees, and that grew to 1750 by 1943. He needed a bigger hangar, so he built this one. In the late 1960s, Brintnell even developed an airplane in this building called '*The Northwest Ranger.*' He received many awards, including the Order of the British Empire in 1946. He was inducted as a Member of Canada's Aviation Hall of Fame in 1976 and had a neighbourhood name after him on the city's northeast side. This hangar was demolished in the spring of 2024.

Norwood School

111 Avenue and 95 Street

This school is the second oldest active in Edmonton after McKay Avenue School. Norwood School opened in February 1909, replacing two structures on the same site since 1906. At that time, enrollment at the two temporary buildings averaged fifty-one students per classroom. Norwood School provided space for four hundred students in ten classrooms over three floors. In its early years, grades one through eight were taught here. Modern for its time, it had indoor toilets and drinking fountains. The Trustees were criticized for building such an expensive school in the "wilderness."

Little has changed structurally since the school was built; a gymnasium was added in the 1960s, and the top floor has become a library. In the 1990s, some major restoration work was done. Norwood School still operates from kindergarten to grade six.

Oberg Block

118 Street and 127 Avenue

The building was constructed by Fredrick Oberg in 1909 in what was then known as West Edmonton.
The Grand Trunk Pacific Railway set up shop here, bringing in hundreds of new jobs and workers. Many built their homes in the area, which saw a boom in population in this part of the city, including the Oberg Block.
The main floor was rented for fifteen dollars a month as a general store known as the Enterprise Store.
This building was one of the area's most defining buildings for several decades. It eventually became a residential property, as it is one of the few remaining heritage buildings in Calder.

Old Scona Academic School

84 Avenue and 105 Street

It was opened in 1908 by Alberta's first premier, Alexander Rutherford, at a cost of just over $86,000. The original name was Strathcona Collegiate Institute, and it was one of the first high schools in the province.

In 1909, university classes were held here while the current campus was constructed. The main floor had four high school classrooms, while the second had four university classrooms. The building continued serving high school and university students until 1911, when the University moved to its current location.

This is Edmonton's oldest active secondary school, and this place received its provincial historic designation one hundred years after it opened in 2008.

Oliver Exchange Building

121 Street and 102 Avenue

Edmonton's first economic boom happened a century ago, and the need for telephone services was high. Four telephone exchange buildings, one in each quadrant of the city, were constructed to fill that need, including this one, built in 1913.

After years of smooth operation, the building underwent a significant expansion in 1949 to cater to the growing demand for telephone service. A major leap was made in 1982 when the old dial equipment was replaced with cutting-edge digital equipment, marking a significant milestone in the building's history.

Today, several small businesses call this home. Renovations took place in 2017, and the city recognizes it as a historic building.

Oliver School

118 Street and 102 Avenue

Between 1903 and 1913, the Edmonton Public School Board built twenty new schools, this being the largest. The original part of the school cost $100,000 and opened in 1911 with two hundred and eighty students in twelve classrooms. This school had all the modern amenities, including indoor plumbing, electric lights, and a rifle range in the basement. The school's first principal had a staff of nine single women, as married women were not allowed to teach.

In 1918, this place was used as a hospital for victims of the Spanish flu epidemic. Twelve new rooms were added in 1928, as this part of the city was quickly growing. A gymnasium was added in 1957.

Kindergarten to grade nine students and the Nellie McClung Girls' School Program are taught here. This school holds the record for Edmonton Public, as two staff members worked here for eighty-five years combined.

Orange Hall #1654

84 Avenue and 103 Street

The Loyal Orange Order was formed in 1795 in Northern Ireland. A decade later, a branch was formed in Canada. Before the government provided social assistance, the church supported families in need. Past members included former Canadian Prime Ministers John A. MacDonald and John Diefenbaker.

Construction on this place started in 1903, and it is one of the oldest surviving public assembly buildings in Alberta. It was established to help pioneer settlers come together as a community and survive the harsh conditions of the new frontier. Today, the Orange Lodge operates primarily to raise funds for children's charities. This place received its historic designation in 2005.

Ortona Armouries

102 Street and 97 Avenue

In 1914, this was the equivalent of today's Amazon warehouse. Hudson Bay Company built this warehouse and stable for its delivery horses, costing $25,000. It was used as a stable until 1924, when the company switched to motorized vehicles. HBC leased its stables to various tenants, including the Edmonton Pure Butter Company. In 1939, it was sold to the Defence Department and used as a Navy training facility for two decades, accommodating more than thirty-seven hundred recruits.

In 1965, it was renamed the Ortona Armouries in commemoration of the regiment's heroic battle of World War II. Later, the building welcomed new tenants such as the Commonwealth Games Association, the National Film Board, the Ortona Gymnastics Club, and the Edmonton Folk Festival. Today, it is called the Ortona Armoury Arts Building. In 2004, the city designated this structure as a historic site.

Outdoor Swimming Pools

The first complete swimming pool opened on August 2, 1922. It was called the South Side Pool before changing the name to the Queen Elizabeth Pool in 1939. Borden Park Pool and Oliver Pool both opened in 1924. These pools were popular. In 1934, 115,000 people attended the three pools. That was when the city's population was just under 80,000. In the mid-1930s, there was an ongoing debate about whether men were allowed to bare their chest while swimming because, at the time, a full-body suit was required.

It took three more decades before another outdoor pool was constructed in the city. The Millcreek Pool was completed in 1953 for $150,000. The last outdoor pool built was the Fred Broadstock Pool in the west end; it opened in 1961. That brings the total to five outdoor pools in the city. Today, the admission for an adult is nine dollars per visit; that was the cost for a season pass in the 1930s. The original Queen Elizabeth pool is gone as of 2004. It was rebuilt in Kinsmen Park, and the Borden Park Pool was modernized at the exact location in 2016.

Our Lady of Mount Carmel School

76 Avenue and 105 Street

This school was constructed in 1925 for $55,000. It had separate entrances for boys and girls from the playground to the six classrooms inside. The building was heated by steam with the heating equipment in the basement.

The architecture drew interest across the country for its practical and well-thought-out design. In 1927, the Royal Canadian Architectural Institute Journal called it a remarkable example of 'modern school planning.' Renovations have happened several times over the life of this century-old structure. The school continues to serve the community's children from kindergarten to grade six.

Paramount Theatre

Jasper Avenue and 102 Street

Construction started in late 1950, as there were some delays in receiving materials, the opening happened in July 1952.

At its inception, the Paramount Theatre boasted a grand seating capacity of over seventeen hundred, making it the largest movie theatre on the Prairies. It was a beacon of luxury in Edmonton, with its plush, comfortable seats and state-of-the-art sound system.

In 1985, the theatre was renovated with a new interior, reducing the seating capacity to eight hundred. 2003, the theatre was sold, and a few years later, it became a church.

Since 2007, the Paramount Theatre has changed hands multiple times, each new owner bringing different plans for its future. The theatre's fate has been uncertain, with proposals ranging from preservation to demolition for the construction of office and condo space.

Parkdale School

85 Street and 116 Avenue

This school was built in 1912 for $100,000. It was all set to open in the spring of 1913, but a fire caused over $10,000 of damage, which delayed the opening by a month.

The gymnasium was moved from the top floor when a new one was constructed in 1957. That space was converted into classrooms.

Over the years, several well-known people attended Parkdale. That would include members of the Edmonton Grads girls' basketball team, who won 502 of 522 games, Dr. Boris Boyko, who was the physician for the Oilers and Eskimos, and W.P. Kinsella, who wrote the novel Shoeless Joe, which inspired the 1989 movie Field of Dreams.

Parkdale School served the community for ninety-seven years before it closed in 2010. The Bent Arrow Traditional Healing Society currently uses the building.

Parkview Apartments

97 Avenue and 106 Street

With a population boom and a housing shortage in the early 1900s, the popularity of apartment living surged. Edmonton saw eighteen new apartment buildings between 1909 and 1915. Compare that to Montreal, which had fifteen apartment houses, and Toronto, which had ten. When this one opened in 1914, the eleven-suite complex was one of the first apartment blocks built in the river valley. The Parkview Apartments was an elegant building attracting many predominant Edmontonians, including teachers, accountants, a city building inspector, an alderman and even an Alberta Supreme Court Judge. As new and modern buildings surround this place, it remains a historically valued property and was given its municipal historic designation in 2002. In 2019, the twenty-seven-storey Symphony Tower was constructed behind Parkview, incorporating the apartment building into their structure, keeping the old alive with the new.

Pendennis Hotel

Jasper Avenue and 96 Street

Pendennis Hotel was the name when construction was completed in 1911. The name has changed several times. The three-storey brick building was recognized as a fine upscale establishment as travellers arrived in Edmonton. When the economy changed due to World War I and prohibition, the hotel was foreclosed on. Stanley Block, a forty-four-unit apartment building, was the new name in 1920. The name changed again in 1945 when it was called Kenmo Lodge and used as a rooming house. 1965 saw the structure sold for $70,000 and was called The Lodge Hotel. Over the next two decades, the building fell into disrepair and was abandoned.

Pendennis is one of the few original buildings built before the First World War that still stands on Jasper Avenue. Developers realized the value of these old gems as this place received a ten-million-dollar facelift after being declared a municipal historic resource in 2001. The name has changed again, this time to the Pendennis Building. With an addition to the back of the building, this place is now office space and available to host events.

Peter Hemingway Pool

111 Avenue and 138 Street

This award-winning pool is located in Coronation Park and was designed by Peter Hemingway. The facility opened in 1970 for $1.2 million and was originally called Coronation Pool. The pool was inspired by one in Tokyo, Japan. It is an Olympic-sized pool, and at the time, was unlike anything ever seen in Edmonton, with its futuristic design. The building shape is the crest of a wave. Hemingway won the Massey Medal for Architecture, the highest honour in the country for architecture.

In 2005, the pool was named after Hemingway to commemorate and honour his work in the Edmonton area, which includes the Muttart Conservatory.

The pool has been closed since 2020 due to the pandemic and scheduled renovations that started a year later. The estimated $46.1M rehabilitation work will upgrade its mechanical, structural, and electrical systems, as well as the exterior and roof.

The scheduled reopening is in 2026, to coincide with the new Coronation Park Sports and Recreation Centre that is being built beside it.

Phillips Building

104 Street and 101 Avenue

Originally named the *Purcell and Kelly Building,* it is a five-story structure located in downtown's warehouse district.

This building was intended to be the first completely fire-proof complex in the city, as the builders used the latest 1912 technology, such as fire-proof doors and windows.

Completion happened during Edmonton's first economic boom in 1913 to store manufactured goods for the city and Northern Alberta.

James Brody bought the building in the early 1950s and renamed it Phillip, after his grandson. This building was to be torn down a couple of times, first in 1981 and again in 2000.

In 2001, a new owner converted the building into lofts, saving this site from becoming a future parking lot. That same year, it was given its municipal historic designation.

Phyllis Grocery Building

96 Street and 106 Avenue

Before we had big box retail outlets, we had corner stores that sold everything you would need. In the 1950s, more than one hundred corner stores were scattered throughout the city, at least a couple in every neighbourhood. Phyllis Grocery is one of those places; not only did you buy penny candies here, but you would get your weekly groceries, and it would also be a meeting place for the neighbours.

As supermarkets started to come to the city in the 1960s, followed by chain stores, there was a lot of pressure on the independents to survive, and many disappeared over the next few decades.

Built in 1941, this may no longer be the area grocery store, but it lives as a pharmacy and was declared a historic building in 2016.

Power Substation #100

80 Street and 115 Avenue

The Edmonton Radial Railway used to operate the power system for the streetcars from a substation in the Boyle Street Community. They had a huge debt of almost $150,000, so on May 1, 1913, The Edmonton Light and Power Company took over the operation. The substation was a small wooden structure on 95 Street that required some work. Instead of fixing the building, a brick substation was constructed on 80 Street. It was designed by Allan Jeffers, the city's first Architect of the new City Architecture Department. It took six months to finish this two-storey place and get it operational. It served the expanding north part of the city, all the way out to the Highlands neighbourhood. It worked well for decades, but as the city kept growing, more and bigger substations were built, and this one eventually closed.

The original wood roof and doors are still in place. Even though the windows have been covered with bricks, this substation still stands as a structure of the city's growth and history.

Prince Charles School

127 Street and 123 Avenue

When this school opened in 1949, it was initially named Sherbrooke School. That only lasted until 1953, when the name was changed to Prince Charles School to honour Queen Elizabeth II's firstborn child.

Soon after, the area residents petitioned the city to have the community name changed to Prince Charles as well. It didn't take long for the enrollment to outgrow this school; six more classrooms were added in 1956 for $71,000. Junior High grades were also in the building for a few years, from 1958 to 1963. Due to budget restraints in 1969, the office secretary had to split her time between two schools.

The principal asked the board for additional help and was denied. As a solution, parents volunteered to work in the office for the school year. Today, this school is home to three hundred students.

Prince of Wales Armouries

108 Avenue and 104 Street

Initially called the Edmonton Drill Hall, it opened on November 17th, 1915. This military training site for the Department of National Defence featured a large drill hall with twenty thousand feet of floor space. It was home to several Battalions and regiments, including the Loyal Edmonton Regiment.

In 1921, the name was changed to the Prince of Wales Armoury. The building continued as an essential facility for the Armed Forces until 1977. The brick castle was showing its age, and a more modern facility at C.F.B. Griesbach was preferred, so the Defense Department abandoned this building. In 1982, the facility became the property of the City of Edmonton.

Today, the Prince of Wales Armouries is a vibrant hub of activity. It houses the City of Edmonton Archives and the Loyal Edmonton Regiment Museum, preserving our city's history. Additionally, it provides unique reception rooms for rent, offering a one-of-a-kind venue for special events.

Princess Theatre

82 Avenue and 103 Street

Construction began weeks before World War I started in 1914. Built by John W. McKernan, a highly successful entrepreneur, he engraved his name on the front of the building, even though it is called the Princess Theatre. It only took ten months and $75,000 to build, with the theatre opening on March 8, 1915. McKernan spent much of the budget on the finishing touches, such as marble, ceramics and stained glass windows. The theatre had a seating capacity for six hundred and sixty moviegoers and was the largest stage in Western Canada. The Princess was more than just a movie theatre; it had a billiards room in the basement with offices and apartments on the third floor.

For twenty-five years, the Princess Theatre was the only theatre south of the river, until 1940 when the Varscona and the Garneau cinemas opened. The Princess ceased to operate as a theatre in 1958, transforming into a space for various retail outlets. However, in 1970, it was reborn as a movie house under the management of different companies. Unfortunately, the doors were closed once more, this time due to the COVID-19 pandemic. Despite these challenges, the Princess Theatre was recognized for its historical importance, receiving a provincial historic designation in May 1995.

Provincial Museum and Archives Building

102 Avenue and 128 Street

The Provincial Archives of Alberta dates back to 1906 when the Provincial Library was established. They collected materials with the idea of preserving them for future generations. In the early days, a small room in the Legislative Building was used as the museum. The collections quickly grew over the years, and by the 1960s, it became one of the largest museums in Western Canada. Since more space was needed, this building was constructed and opened in 1967 as a part of Canada's Centennial celebrations.

In the 1990s, the Provincial Archives had so much in their collection they had to store a lot of it offsite. In 2003, the Archives built a new 118,000-square-foot home on Roper Road. In 2005, Queen Elizabeth II visited Alberta for the province's 100th birthday, and this place was renamed the Royal Alberta Museum. In 2011, a decision was made to build a new museum downtown. Before the doors closed in 2015, a forty-eight-hour closing party was held to celebrate forty-eight years at this location. Over 35,000 people came out to visit one last time.

Queen Alexandra School

106 Street and 77 Avenue

When this school opened, it was in the Town of Strathcona; today, it is Edmonton's oldest continuously operating school. It cost $27,000 to build and opened in 1906. It was originally named Duggan Street School after J.J. Duggan, a former alderman and mayor of Strathcona. In 1910, it was renamed Queen Alexandra.

In 1908, the third-floor assembly hall served as a temporary lecture hall for students attending the newly formed University of Alberta. There have been alterations and additions over the years, but the heart of the original structure still stands. Approximately one hundred and seventy-five students from kindergarten to grade six attend.

Queen Elizabeth II Planetarium

In Coronation Park by 142 Street and 111 Avenue

Construction of the Queen Elizabeth II Planetarium commenced after the esteemed visit of Queen Elizabeth II and Prince Phillip to Edmonton in 1959. The grand opening on September 23, 1960, amidst the massive interest in the space race, was a momentous occasion, marking a significant milestone in the city's history.

At its grand opening, the Queen Elizabeth II Planetarium was a trailblazer, being the first municipal Planetarium in Canada. Its popularity soared, with over 33,000 people visiting in 1967.

It closed at the end of 1983 when the much bigger Space and Science Centre opened a few months later. The Planetarium sat empty for many years. The value of the building was realized, and it received its municipal historic designation in 2017. In the early 2020s, restoration of this facility, a painstaking process that involved preserving its original design and features, happened. The second grand opening of this building was held in October 2023. The city still owns the Planetarium, which they lease to the Telus World of Science to host various events.

Rat Hole

109 Street and 104 Avenue

Before there was an intersection at this location, the 109 Street Tunnel was here, or as everyone called it, The Rat Hole. A former city alderman coined the name, and it stuck. If you are unfamiliar with Rat Hole, it was a five hundred and fifty-one foot tunnel on 109 Street. It was between 104-105 Avenues, under twenty-two tracks of the Canadian National Rail Yard that used to be downtown, from 101-116 streets. Built in 1927, it opened in October 1928 with one lane northbound and one lane southbound. At its peak, 27,000 vehicles used it every day. A twin tunnel was to be constructed to help with the increase in traffic, but it was never built. When CN Rail moved its tracks out of downtown, the tunnel was demolished in 2000. The cement from the tunnel was used as the fill-in to build the road. From start to finish, this project only took three months and finished twenty-five days ahead of schedule!

Remax Field / Diamond Park

Rossdale Road and 98 Avenue

This area has a rich baseball history dating back to 1884. It gained more interest with the construction of Diamond Park. It had 1,500 seats and a covered grandstand, built by a local businessman, Frank Gray, Edmonton's baseball club director, in 1907. As the sport's popularity grew, Renfrew Park was constructed across the field in 1935 to replace Diamond Park as Edmonton's main field. It held that name for forty-five years when it was renamed John Ducey Park in 1980. This was to honour Edmonton's "Mr. Baseball," who started as a batboy, then a player, an umpire and a sports reporter for the Edmonton Bulletin.

John Ducey Park had 6,500 seats and was the home field for the AAA Edmonton Trappers of the Pacific Coast League from 1981 to 2004.

After six decades of witnessing the highs and lows of the game, the iconic John Ducey Park made way for a new era in 1995. In its place, a modern park emerged, boasting a larger seating capacity of 9,200 and thirty executive suites. This new park, a symbol of growth and evolution, was christened Telus Field, now known as RE/MAX Field.

Revillon Building

104 Street and 102 Avenue

The original part of the Revillon Building was constructed in 1908. A six-storey tower was added in 1912 for $300,000. This was one of the most modern buildings in the city, with electric hoists, an elevator, telephones and pneumatic tubes.

It was built for the Revillion family as they expanded from France to North America. Edmonton became their headquarters of operations in Western Canada. By 1912, they had ninety-six stores throughout the country. They dealt in hardware, dry goods and groceries. The company completed the sale of their business to the Hudson's Bay Company by 1936. The building sold several times, including to J.W. Ashdown Hardware. In 1949, this was the scene of Edmonton's largest fire. It took two days to extinguish because of the steel and concrete construction. The walls and beams remained standing, only the contents burned. Renovations happened in 1971 and 1986 thats when the back alley was closed. An atrium connected with the Boardwalk Building. More renovations occurred from 2019 to 2024. Today, this complex is called the Revillon Boardwalk Building, and both structures have received their historic designation from the city. The oldest operating freight elevator in Edmonton is still in use.

Richards Block

82 Avenue and 104 Street

The A.H. Richards and Company general store has a solid foundation, two-foot-thick walls, and steel reinforcement. It cost $30,000 to build, and when it opened in 1910, there was great fanfare, an orchestra played all day, and special discounts were offered on all items in the store.

On the ground level, they sold various products, including clothing, household items, and groceries. The upper floors originally had many uses, such as a dance hall, offices, and meeting rooms, but in 1926, they were converted to apartments.

Many businesses have occupied the main floor over the last century, as it remains a vibrant hub in Old Strathcona. This place received its historic designation in 1976.

Ring House's

Saskatchewan Drive and 115 Street

Between 1911 and 1914, a cluster of ten two-storey brick houses formed a ring on the northwest corner of the University of Alberta campus. The houses were initially built to accommodate the esteemed faculty. Notably, Ring House number one, the second oldest building at the U of A, was the residence of five of the University's Presidents from 1912 to 1959.

This particular house is the oldest President's residence anywhere in Canada. The remaining Ring Houses have been home to other University leaders, professors and deans.

Over the years, the Ring Houses have been versatile in their use. They have served as the Museum and Collections Service, the University of Alberta Press, and even as a daycare from 1969 to 2010. Ring House's number five to ten were demolished in 1970, with the others left standing. In 2021, the University announced that the remaining four Ring Houses would be torn down later in the year, as they no longer support the institution's needs and have high maintenance costs. A petition with over 2,300 signatures called on the U of A to suspend its plans to demolish the houses; in response to the public outcry, the U of A has offered to sell each of the buildings for one dollar each if buyers agree to pay the moving costs. A development group stepped forward to dismantle the houses, but there is no word on when or where they will be rebuilt. Alberta does not have legislation for the heritage designation of buildings on post-secondary campuses.

Ritchie Mill

Saskatchewan Drive and 101 Street

Constructed in 1892, the same year the railroad arrived, Robert Ritchie built the mill at the end of the rail line and began operating a flour mill. Elevators were added in 1895 and 1902.

Ritchie, a prominent figure, also served in local politics as an alderman, school trustee, justice of the peace, and Mayor of Strathcona. This building functioned as a flour mill until 1948. As of 2012, it had been converted into an office and retail building. It is the oldest surviving flour mill building in the province.

Some parts of the mill were torn down what remains received their Provincial Historic designation in 1979 and their Municipal designation in 1997.

Riverdale Neighborhood

99 to 103 A Avenue and 87 to 95 Street

In the late 1800s, along the North Saskatchewan River, this area was an inexpensive part of the city to live in. That attracted many newcomers to settle here. They worked at the nearby Brickyard and lived in tiny brick houses constructed of discarded bricks. They had no electricity, water, or sewage lines.

This community soon became known as Dogpatch. Families raised kids, grew vegetables, and maintained a distinct, independent community. They even traded amongst themselves. For a short time, they had their own currency. As the area prospered, the name changed to the Riverdale Neighbourhood in 1920.

Dogpatch, which had a rich history of almost one hundred years, was shut down by the city in 1985 due to health code concerns, particularly related to the lack of basic amenities.

Today, the memories of Dogpatch live on in the area. There is a pub named after the community and a housing area called Brickyard. The area has undergone significant changes since the closure of Dogpatch, with some parts being transformed into modern developments while others have been preserved to honour the history.

Riverdale School

101 Avenue and 89 Street

The original school was built in 1913. It consisted of three buildings until 1922 when they became too small for the number of students. J.B. Little, who owned a brickyard in the area, donated the land and the bricks to build this new structure in 1923. The final cost of construction was $3,620. The Principal at the time, Janet Harley, led her students from the old school to the new, big, brand-new one. Behind her was a parade of students carrying desks, books and the rest of the school's materials. Janet Harley had education in her blood, as she was a teacher for sixty-five years, including nineteen years at Riverdale as the Principal.

The school is one of the longest-operating in the city; it celebrated its one-hundredth anniversary in 2023.

Robertson-Wesley United Church

102 Avenue and 123 Street

The Robertson-Presbyterian Church was built in 1913 for $110,000. It was named after Reverend James Robertson, the Superintendent of Missions in western Canada.

In 1925, a significant chapter in the church's history was written when the membership voted to become a United Church. Another name change happened forty-six years later, in 1971, when they merged with the Wesley United Church.

For decades, the massive octagonal spire marked Edmonton's western edge. The first Sunday service in this building was on January 25th, 1914, just months before World War I started. To this day, in the Memorial Hall inside, they commemorate the sacrifice made by the church members during the Second World War; two hundred and ninety-seven enlisted and twenty-eight died. The church was declared an Edmonton heritage building in 1989.

Ross Flats Apartments

101 Street and 95 Avenue

Set in one of Edmonton's oldest neighbourhoods, Rossdale, this building has worn many hats. Originally a Children's Shelter, it transitioned into Grace Hospital, operated by the Salvation Army. It even served as a refuge for children from 1936 to 1942. Such a diverse history is a testament to its enduring significance.

During the Second World War, it was converted to housing for American soldiers working on the Alaska Highway, which led to its nickname, "Little American Transit Hotel." After the war, it was turned into the Ross Flats apartments. So few buildings have been home to such a variety of people. The City of Edmonton still owns the property. It was designated a historical building in 2001.

Ross Sheppard High School

111 Avenue and 135 Street

It was named after Ross Sheppard, who had a forty-two-year career with Edmonton Public Schools as a teacher, principal, and the fourth superintendent of the school board. Before that, he was an athlete, representing Canada in the 1924 Paris Olympic Games. He also set a Canadian record for the standing high jump, which he held for forty-four years!

The school opened in 1957 for two million dollars. The iconic totem pole didn't take its position in front of the building until 1967 as a centennial project. The forty-two-foot log weighs 7500 pounds and was carved in the gymnasium over a six-week time frame. One of the more notable students who attended here was Wayne Gretzky after he was traded to the Oilers. The school's enrollment has grown from 893 students to just under 2300.

Rossdale Brewery Building

100 Street 98 Avenue

Rossdale Brewery is the oldest standing brewery in Edmonton and the oldest standing unaltered brewery in the province. It was built in 1905 by the owner of the Strathcona Hotel when the brewing industry flourished in Alberta.

By 1908, the annual production was estimated at 20,000 barrels, distributed to bars across north-central Alberta. With the demand for beer growing, the business was so successful that the company moved to a larger building.

A new brewery was built on 104th Avenue and 121 Street in 1913, now known as Brewery District.

When prohibition started in Alberta in 1917, the brewery in Rossdale eventually closed, and the property was sold. It was used for various businesses, including storage and a garage, until the 1970s. A proposed plan to turn this place into a condo building is being considered.

Roxy Theatre

124 Street and 107 Avenue

When it opened in 1938, the Roxy was the only theatre in the city west of 104 Street. Glowing reviews by the Edmonton Bulletin Newspaper, which wrote, "Smartly modern in design, eye-catching neon sign, fully air-conditioned." Attending the opening reception were many prominent Edmontonians, including Mayor John Wesley Fry and Lieutenant Governor John C. Bowen. The theatre underwent a major renovation in the 1970s.

The Roxy Theatre was the brainchild of Bill Wilson, the son of long-time Capitol Theatre manager Walter Wilson. After Bill lost his government job during the Depression, he fell back to the family business and, with the help of investors, built the Roxy Theatre. Bill left in 1941 to manage the Garneau Theatre, and the Roxy was bought by Odeon Theatres, who operated it until the 1980s. The Roxy continued as a theatre until finally closing in 1988. The following year, it was purchased by the Theatre Network and transformed into a live performance space. By eliminating some of the seating, adding dressing rooms, and extending the stage and lobby, the Roxy found a new niche within Edmonton. The Roxy thrived until January 2015, when the theatre was destroyed by fire. Much hard work paid off as the theatre was rebuilt at the exact location. The grand reopening occurred on April 14, 2022.

Royal Lawn Bowling Club

On the Alberta Legislature Grounds

This sport originated in ancient Egypt and has been played in England since the thirteenth century. In the mid-nineteenth century, Scotland popularized the sport and drew up rules that remain mostly unchanged today.

The beginnings of this sport in Alberta started at Government House on 102 Avenue in 1923 before moving to its current location on the Alberta Legislative Grounds three years later. In 1935, a second green was added which has since been closed. The existing clubhouse was built in 1959 to commemorate the Queen's visit to the province. Several firsts have taken place here over the years.

The first "mixed" tournament was held between men and women in 1937. In 1960, the Royal hosted the Canadian Championship. 1962 was the first year it was legal to play on a Sunday, and 1991 was the first Provincial Tournament for the Blind. On July 9, 2023, the club celebrated its one-hundredth anniversary and will continue to go strong for the next one hundred years.

Rundle Park

113 Avenue and 29 Street

This space was many things before it became a park. The area in the Village of Beverly started as a farm, then coal was discovered, and it was sold to Humberstone Mine Company in 1900. The company slogan was "Fill your bins with our coal—The Best Coal Mined!" In the busy winter season, they had a capacity of ten tons of coal daily and two hundred employees.

Over the mine's life, the workers pulled almost one million tons of coal from the ground before it closed in 1934. As the coal reserves depleted, the mine was sealed.

Before the Town of Beverly amalgamated with Edmonton, this area was their landfill until The City of Edmonton bought it in 1956 for just under $30,000. The dump site would reach maximum capacity within fifteen years. Which in turn gave us this park by the mid-1970s.

Rutherford House

Saskatchewan Drive and 112 Street

This beautiful mansion was named after Alexander Rutherford, who lived here after construction in 1911. It is one of the oldest houses in the Garneau neighbourhood.

Not only was he the province's first premier from 1905 to 1910, but Rutherford was also a lawyer and a key figure in establishing the University of Alberta. He used his home to entertain visitors of the province and the University.

The Rutherfords sold their home and furnishings in 1940 to a fraternity, which converted it into a frat house. This place was almost bulldozed to make way for a new development in 1966.

After plenty of public outcry, the house was saved and restored to its former glory. In 1975, it received its provincial historic designation and became a museum that celebrates the life of Alberta's first Premier.

Rutherford School

91 Street and 86 Avenue

It is named after Alberta's first Premier, Alexander Rutherford. This school opened in 1911 for $17,000. Initially, the school had only four rooms before additions in 1914, 1916, and 1957. The school only had twenty principals, and the first one, Maude Bell, was quite the pioneer. Not only because she was a female principal at a time when that didn't occur very often, but she held that position for thirty years. She was also really resourceful. She didn't receive any sports equipment from the school board. Just like today, they had to do a fundraiser. So she had the field on the west side of the school plowed and had the children plant potatoes in the spring and harvest them in the fall; in turn, she sold the crop and had enough money to buy the needed sports equipment. The school is still an important fixture in the neighbourhood, as it is open to 263 students from kindergarten to grade six.

Sacred Heart Church

96 Street and 108 Avenue

Construction began on May 15, 1913. The estimated cost was $50,000, and the money was raised by the congregation. It only took seven months to build this place, as they held their first mass on Christmas Day.

This structure certainly has had its ups and downs. In the 1970s, they held volunteer-run free Christmas dinners. In the 1980s, a food bank started operating out of the basement.

On the downside, in 1966, a three-alarm fire took four hours to put out. An eight-year-old boy playing with matches caused $200,000 worth of damage.

Another rebuild happened after a second major fire in 2020. Construction crews worked overtime to get as much done as possible before the Pope visited this place on July 25, 2022.

Salvation Army Citadel

102 Street and 100 Avenue

Starting as The Christian Mission in London, England, in 1865, it was re-named The Salvation Army in 1878. The Salvation Army began its work in Canada in 1882. They held their first church services in Edmonton in 1893. After moving multiple times, they settled at this permanent location. Built in 1925, it served as a church, a meeting hall, and one of the city's leading social service agencies for forty years. In 1965, it sold for $100,000 and converted to house the city's first professional live theatre. It stayed here until the new Citadel Theatre opened near City Hall in 1976. Since then, this place has seen various uses as a Beauty School, commercial ventures, and concert venues. So far, this place is only on the municipal list waiting for its historic designation.

Scona Garage & Apartments

105 Street and 81 Avenue

One of Edmonton's first car dealerships and 'motor hospitals.' When it opened in 1912, the building cost $40,000. The second floor was designed as apartments, while the main floor was an automotive dealership and service centre selling Cadillac and Dodge. It was large enough to store sixty-five automobiles. In 1914, approximately one hundred vehicles were on city streets. A year later, in 1915, the sales centre closed, and it became just a repair shop.

Over the years, the building has undergone several transformations. It continued as a garage and apartment until 1974 when the ground floor became a restaurant and the second floor became storage. The Keg Steakhouse occupied the space for forty-five years, adding another layer to the building's rich history. In 2019, they moved out, marking yet another transformation.

Renovations are happening on the upper floor to create a hotel and retail outlets on the ground level. The building received its historic designation in 2006.

Sheppard Block

82 Avenue and 103 Street

William Sheppard came to Edmonton in 1894, managing and owning several hotels. He became a politician, serving on the first Strathcona Council in 1899. He was also involved with Edmonton's growing brewing industry, building breweries in 1904 and 1913, and in the midst of that, he was elected mayor of Strathcona in 1906.

He wasn't busy enough, so he built the Sheppard Block in 1907. Today, over twenty-four thousand vehicles drive by daily and likely don't notice this structure, which blends in with the other buildings along this strip.

Committed to Strathcona, Sheppard built his thirty-five hundred square-foot home nearby in 1911 for eight thousand dollars. The National Film Board used his house for a set, and it was designated a provincial historic building in 1981.

Sheriff Robertson Park

82 Street and 111 Avenue

This park was named after Walter Scott Robertson, born in New Brunswick in 1841. He came to Edmonton in 1881 and established a general store before getting involved in the local real estate market. Three years later, he was appointed Deputy Sheriff. He was also musically talented. He built Edmonton's first theatre and opera house in 1893. When Alberta became a Province in 1905, the same year Robertson became Sheriff, he located his office in the opera house. It was only there for one year, as it burned down in 1906.

In 1912, Sheriff Robertson constructed his retirement home a few blocks from this park, overlooking the North Saskatchewan River. The cost was $10,000. It was one of the first houses in the Cromdale neighbourhood, a beautiful home with a fireplace, elegant furnishings, mouldings, and trims. Robertson didn't live there very long; he passed away of natural causes in 1915 at the age of seventy-four. His house did get its provincial historic designation in 1987.

Shop-Easy Grocery

129 Avenue and 116 Street

The Shop Easy store opened in 1948 as a local grocery store in the Calder area. Quickly, it became a community hub where locals would buy their groceries, have a snack and catch up with their fellow neighbours, making it a central part of daily life in Calder.

By the late 1950s, an addition was constructed on the west side of the building. Not seeing the grocery shift, in the 1960s, larger grocery stores came to Edmonton, and many local shops like this would be closed, as they could not compete.

While the Shop-Easy Grocery store may no longer be in operation, its legacy lives on. Over the years, it has housed various businesses and adapted to the changing needs of the community. After the building received its historic designation in 2016, this place was re-imaged. A second storey was added to accompany apartments and retail on the main level.

Smith Crossing Bridge

23 Avenue and 125 Street

The original bridge was built in the early 1900s and named after Robert and Elizabeth Smith. They were pioneers in preserving this area, as they lived nearby with their family for seventy-three years. The bridge was initially built for vehicles over Whitemud Creek but changed to a pedestrian bridge in 1961. As the structure aged, it wore out and needed to be replaced. Construction started in November 2022 and finished in September 2023.

The projected cost of the new bridge was about two and a half to three million dollars, and the final price tag was $6.3 million.

Spruce Avenue School

102 Street and 114 Avenue

The original school was a wooden framed building that was constructed in 1917. It lasted for twelve years before this one opened in 1929. This structure cost $150,000 to build, and since it was named Spruce Avenue School, the principal thought it was a great idea to plant two spruce trees in front of the school to commemorate the opening. The only problem is that once the trees started to grow, it was discovered that they had mistakenly planted pine trees. In 1954, an addition to the school happened as they did correct the error and had another tree-planting ceremony.

Almost a decade after opening, the school is still going strong, with more than two hundred students walking through the doors.

St. Albert/Edmonton Transit System

A century ago, St. Albert Trail was an unpaved road; it was impassable when conditions were wet and muddy. On September 1, 1913, service began with an inter-urban railway between St. Albert and the Town of Calder. The train was a gasoline/electric streetcar that took 30 minutes to complete the route, with a few stops in between. But it only lasted six months, when service abruptly ended on April 1, 1914, when a fire destroyed the train storage garage. The service never resumed. After three years of debate, local politicians decided not to continue the train in favour of private buses. That happened for the next few decades until Edmonton Transit was contracted for bus service in 1974, followed by St. Albert purchasing ten transit buses in 1976. St. Albert Transit added to their fleet and built a garage to store them.

St. Albert Transit was at the forefront with many firsts. Such as the first system in Western Canada to own and operate the accordion buses, the low-floor wheelchair-accessible buses, and the first transit system in Alberta to introduce real-time bus arrival information.

Today, they operate sixty-three buses, with a ridership of over one and a quarter million passengers annually.

St. Anthony School

84 Avenue and 104 Street

Before St. Anthony School was built, students attended a one-room school at a nearby church. Constructed in 1906, this was the first Catholic school south of the river.

As the population grew, more space was needed, and additions were made. When enrollment declined, the doors were closed to students in 1973. Since then, Edmonton Catholic Schools has used it as a meeting centre, storage facility, and archives. They are consolidating administrative buildings to save money and are trying to sell this place for $6.6 million.

The city has placed a plaque on the building, acknowledging its history, but it does not have a historical designation.

St. Joachim Church

110 Street and 99 Avenue

This church is one of the oldest buildings in the city and also the oldest Roman Catholic parish in Edmonton. This church is a testament to the city's rich history, dating back to the groundbreaking ceremony on December 8, 1898. After raising $16,000, construction started, and the first service happened one year later. The steeple was added in 1901, and the vestry was finished in 1912. St. Joachim is one of the earliest and most impressive Roman Catholic churches in the province. It has served as a model for several others around Alberta.

The church received its provincial historic designation in 1978 and a municipal one in 2018.

St. Josaphat Ukrainian Church

97 Street and 108 Avenue

The original church was built at this site in 1904 and only lasted a few decades before it became too small for the congregation. Construction started on this structure in 1939, and there were a few reasons why it took eight years to complete, including financial ones. But this place did open on June 3, 1947, for $250,000. It was nicknamed the "Prairie Cathedral". The church was well attended, as Edmonton's Ukrainian population grew from about 6,000 in 1941 to over 84,000 in 1981.

St. Josaphat Ukrainian Church, described in a 1953 London England newspaper, was a "vibrant hub of Ukrainian culture," earning the area "a Little Europe." It was a place where English was a minority language, a testament to the strong Ukrainian community that had formed. This cultural haven, a rendezvous for new Canadians immigrating from Europe, remained a popular spot. In 1964, a new Rectory was built to meet the growing needs of the parish. This place received its historic designation first by the province in 1983 and then by the city in 2015, in preserving and promoting Ukrainian culture.

St. Joseph's Basilica

Jasper Avenue and 113 Street

The ground was broken in 1913, taking fifty years to complete. There were a few reasons for the delays, such as financial troubles, two World Wars, and the great depression. With the start and stop cycles of construction, repairs were needed, as problems with the foundation were discovered. Work started again in 1960 to finish the project on this twelve-hundred-seat structure. The grand opening ceremony happened on May 1, 1963. The cathedral was known as a "church without locks," as it was open twenty-four hours a day. That changed in 1980, as an arsonist set the altar on fire, causing $250,000 of damage. It took seventeen months to do the repairs, ending the open-door policy.

Pope John Paul II visited Edmonton as part of the papal visit, a significant event that drew thousands of people to the basilica. Many long-time Edmontonians will remember that this is where Wayne Gretzky, the legendary hockey player, married back in 1988, adding another chapter to the basilica's rich history.

St. Joseph's College

89 Avenue and 114 Street

Alberta needed Catholic post-secondary education, so the Province established St. Joseph's College in 1926, constructing and opening this building one year later.

At the start, the College had up to one hundred men living in small dorm rooms and taking university courses. The Chapel was very poorly heated compared to the rest of the building, so in winter, the students would wear toques to stay warm.

A swimming pool was to be constructed inside. But after a protest, fearing men and women might swim together, the space was turned into a gymnasium.

There are now sixty-three men in residence, with a separate women's building housing two hundred and eighty-four.

Former Prime Minister Joe Clark was one of the more notable students who graduated from St. Joseph.

St. Joseph's Hospital

82 Avenue and 108 Street

The hospital opened its doors in 1948 at a cost of about $700,000. The original building had one hundred and fifty beds over four floors. In 1955, the hospital took a significant step in its growth and service to the community as two additional storeys were added, expanding its capacity to serve. It continued to serve the community for many decades until it was closed in 1993, ending an era.

After sitting vacant for several years, the building underwent a remarkable transformation. A seventh floor and balconies were added, and in 1997, it came alive again as The Garneau Lofts. The building, once a symbol of healthcare, now houses a mix of businesses on the ground floor and residential suites on the other five floors. This place received its municipal historic designation in 1994.

St. Stephen's College

112 Street and 88 Avenue

Known initially as Alberta College South, it was completed in 1911 and was the first building on the University of Alberta campus.

The Alberta College South building was a college and residence, with forty-one students enrolled in the Faculty of Theology.

The building was also a recovery hospital during the First World War. In 1935, a chapel was added and remains today. The new St. Stephen's College building was built next to this one in 1952. After avoiding demolition in 1977, the provincial government purchased the building, restored it, and made it the home of the Province's Historical Resources Division. Ironically, this place has no historic recognition.

Stanley A. Milner Library

102 Avenue and 100 Street

When it opened in 1967, it was called the Centennial Library and renamed in 1996 to honour Stanley Albert Milner for his lifetime of commitment to Edmonton Public Library. He was the chair of the EPL Board from 1963 until 1968. Before that, he received a science degree from the University of Alberta and served in the military; he was a businessman, an oilfield pioneer, and a city council member. Milner served on many boards, including the Edmonton Community Foundation, Northlands, The Eskimo Football Club, the Edmonton Symphony Orchestra, Junior Achievement, the Salvation Army and the United Way. Milner also received the Alberta Order of Excellence.

The Library closed for renovations in January 2017 and reopened in September 2020. It receives over 1.2 million visits each year. Mr. Milner passed away in 2021 at the age of ninety-one.

Steele Heights Junior High School

59 Street and 146 Avenue

The school opened in 1968 for $975,000. It is named after Sir Samuel Benfield Steele, a distinguished Canadian soldier, the commanding officer of Strathcona's Horse, and an officer in the newly formed North West Mounted Police during the Klondike Gold Rush in the Yukon.

Portables were added in the late 1970s and early 1980s, as this school has always had a high enrollment. Even today, over five hundred students attend. Shortly after the school opened, an additional $16,300 was needed to install folding partitions in the gym to create two more teaching areas and to install clocks in the classrooms.

Not only does this school bear Sam Steele's name, but the Edmonton Garrison is also known as the Steele Barracks. In the Yukon, Canada's fifth-highest mountain is called Mount Steele.

Stovel Block

97 Street and 103 Avenue

It was named after James Stovel, one of the first hardware merchants in Edmonton. His wife, Mary, supervised the construction of this place for two years until its completion in 1912. Apartments were on the upper floors, and stores were on the ground level, including Armstrong Drug Store, named after George Armstrong, the owner and Edmonton's eleventh mayor.

Over the years, this building has been home to various other businesses, including a Loans and Exchange store, a Pawnbroker, and a diner. Although it has been empty for a few years, it has a second lease on life as it was bought and renovated as a women's transitional home.

It became a city-designated historic site in 2019.

Strand Hotel

127 Avenue and 120 Street

It was built in the Village of Calder in 1912, originally at 129 Avenue and 123 Street, for $50,000. The hotel was promoted as having some of the finest amenities, including all forty rooms being "good rooms with hot and cold water" and fireproof.

By 1927, the owners felt they needed a better location, so they raised and moved the building five blocks to its current spot on 127 Avenue and 120 Street, adjacent to the rail yard, to accommodate more traffic. Renamed the Dover Hotel in 1951, it has served the local community ever since.

Strathcona Hotel

82 Avenue and Gateway Boulevard

The hotel is the oldest commercial structure in the city. It was built at the "end of the line" by the Calgary and Edmonton Railway Company in 1891. It was expanded several times, first in 1903 and again in 1907. It was the largest hotel in the region for over a decade.

Most of the hotel's revenue came from the tavern, and when prohibition occurred, the hotel was sold to the Presbyterian Church. It was used for the Westminster Ladies College from 1918 to 1924. As prohibition ended, the building was converted back to a hotel.

The building underwent further renovations in the 2010s. The tavern is now open again, with Leopold's occupying the main floor. This place received its historical designation in 2001.

Strathcona Library

104 Street and 83 Avenue

The Strathcona Library opened in March 1913 for $27,000. It is the oldest surviving public library in Edmonton and one of the oldest in the province. The basement was a men's reading room, while the second-floor auditorium was a community focal point where the Edmonton Medical Association and the Ladies Hospital League met. The first renovation happened in 1948, converting the basement into a children's library.

By the late 1960s, the building needed to be better maintained and began showing its age, as the second floor could no longer support the weight of books. Edmonton Public Library attempted to close the branch in 1970, but public opposition was able to keep it open.

In 1984, the library received a $250,000 restoration. Since the mid-1980s, the branch has become one of Edmonton Public's busiest libraries. This building was recognized as a provincial historic building in 2006.

Strathcona Public Building

82 Avenue and 105 Street

Construction of the Strathcona Public Building began in 1911. Despite several delays, the building was completed in two years. The federal government intended the use of this place as the Post Office, Customs, and Inland Revenue Bureau. The building served as the Post Office until 1977, a significant part of its historical uses.

The Strathcona Public Building was granted provincial historic designation in 1985. A year later, the City of Edmonton took ownership, leasing it to transform it into a vibrant public space that became home to a restaurant, bar, and billiards club.

Strathcona Roundhouse

100 Street and 77 Avenue

Here are the remnants of the roundhouse. The purpose of the early train roundhouses was to store and turn locomotives around. This roundhouse consisted of twelve stalls and a turntable, constructed in 1907. It was built at this location because the town of Strathcona feared the trains would cruise past them across the river to Edmonton when the High Level Bridge was constructed. Strathcona agreed to donate seventy acres of land and no property tax for fifteen years if the Canadian Pacific Railway would build at this location to ensure the trains kept this a vital stop. CP agreed and spent fifty thousand dollars to develop this yard, which included the roundhouse.

As the decades passed, this place was used less for locomotive maintenance, so the turntable was removed and replaced with a wye track. A section of the building was torn down, but the other part is still used today for minor repairs.

Strathcona Science Provincial Park

17 Street and 109 Avenue

The land in this area has undergone a remarkable transformation. It started in 1911 as a coal mine for forty-two years, then became a gravel pit and a landfill. At one point, twelve mines were within the park's boundaries. However, in the 1970s, the land was reclaimed as part of the Capital City Recreation Plan. The Science Park opened in 1980 and was Edmonton's most significant archaeological site. They unearthed approximately 25,000 pieces, including pottery, bones, and tools dating back as much as 4500 years.

Four buildings showcased Edmonton's natural resource history, but due to budget shortfalls, this park was only open for eight years before it closed in 1988.

Thousands of pieces showing Edmonton's pre-settlement past, a treasure trove of history, are carefully preserved in the Royal Alberta Museum's vaults. All thanks to the crucial role of the Strathcona Science Provincial Park in preserving Edmonton's heritage.

Due to environmental concerns, this area only offers a limited range of day-use recreational activities, including walking, mountain biking, downhill skiing, and a remote-controlled aircraft park.

Strathcona Telephone Exchange Building

83 Avenue and 104 Street

The first documented telephone connection was made in 1891. By 1895, there were seven phones in Strathcona; by 1901, there were twenty-five. A larger facility was needed, so this building was constructed in 1908.

The ground floor and basement were initially used for equipment and offices, while the second, which is no longer there, provided accommodation for the telephone operator. Over the years, the telephone exchange has seen many changes in equipment.

Edmonton Telephones opened a Historical Information Centre in this building from 1987 to 2004. Today, Telus still operates the Strathcona Telephone Exchange, waiting to be designated a municipal historic building.

Street Railway Substation No. 600

124 Street and 107 Avenue

As the streetcar line extended to the west end, construction took place in 1938 to house equipment to boost power for the street railway cars. It only took three months to build and cost $25,000. Ten years later, the Edmonton City Council decided to eliminate the streetcars in favour of trolleybuses. This building then serviced the trolleybus system until 2009.

A new addition to the back of the building happened, and a pedway connected the building to the south to complete a collection of boutique retail stores, a microbrewery, a restaurant, and offices. This place received its municipal historic designation in 2017.

Telus World of Science

111 Avenue and 142 Street

Construction started in 1982, opening on July 1, 1984. It was constructed to replace the much smaller Planetarium built in 1960. This place has expanded a number of times, in 1992, then in 2001, 2016 and 2022, as a forty million dollar addition. The science centre is not just a place to visit but a place to actively engage with science. You can peer through a telescope at a solar eclipse, interact with numerous displays, attend a laser show, watch an Imax film on the largest screen in Alberta, and conduct a science experiment. It's a hub of interactive learning. When Canadian astronaut Chris Hatfield was on the space station, he held a question and answer session with school kids at this facility. Prime Ministers have visited here; funding has come from all levels of government and private donations, and a non-profit organization operates it.

Thistle Curling Building

114 Avenue and 69 Street

The Thistle is the oldest curling Club in the city. It started in the downtown area in 1920 and moved to the Edmonton Exhibition Grounds near this location.

The Club has faced much turmoil over the last century. During the depression, it operated with a small membership. Then, during World War II, the Royal Canadian Air Force took over the building and used it for war purposes.

By the early 1950s, the Club wanted a new home. They had problems at this location during construction. Strong winds blew down concrete walls and trusses. Then, a plumbers' strike delayed the installation of the pipes. Finally, the official grand opening happened here on January 10, 1953. Five years later, the Thistle was home to three hundred and twenty curlers; decades later, the Club is still striving and producing City Champions, Provincial Champions, Canadian and World Champion winning teams.

Tipton and Hulbert Block

82 Avenue by 104 Street

Russell Hulbert came to Strathcona from Nova Scotia in 1893. The arrival of the railway the year before made him realize the area's importance. He was a grocer, a contractor and a member of the first town council of Strathcona.

On the left, the Tipton was constructed in 1911 and sold a year later for $40,000 to John Tipton, hence the name. In 1912, the Hulbert Block was added for $25,000. Like many of these early buildings, it had retail on the main floor and apartment-style residents above. The building is important because of its connection to the early development of Strathcona.

Numerous businesses have occupied these two buildings over the century it has been here, including the long-time home of Block 1912 cafe and bakery. In 1979, the Tipton received a $400,000 renovation, and both buildings received their municipal historic designation in 2016.

Tony's Pizza Palace

111 Avenue and 96 Street

Tony Mazzotta moved to Canada in 1959 and worked at various hotels, including the Hotel Macdonald. He moved to New York in 1965 and opened his first pizza place in the Bronx. He found success with the family recipe he brought from Italy to New York and opened two more restaurants. Tony moved back to Edmonton in 1974, opening a pizza shop on 118 Avenue by the Coliseum.

Since moving to this location in 1986, Tony's Pizza Palace has been a pillar of the Norwood community. Today, Sal and Tony Junior continue the tradition, keeping their customers satisfied with their delicious pizzas.

Believe it or not, Edmonton is a top city for pizza. According to the Conde Nast Traveler website, in a 2016 survey, the city was ranked number eight globally. Leading the local list is Tony's Pizza Palace. Try their pizza with takeout, delivery, or on their covered patio.

Traffic Circles

142 Street and 107 Avenue

Noel Buckland Dant moved to Edmonton in 1949. He was an urban planner for the city. He had new ideas about how the city should grow, including traffic movement. In 1945, 130,000 vehicles were registered in Alberta; six years later, with the discovery of oil, there were over 250,000. Dant responded by constructing traffic circles to keep vehicles moving efficiently.

He was responsible for the initial twelve traffic circles built in the 1950s. The first was at 111 Avenue and Groat Road and converted to an intersection in 1989. Over the years, drivers had difficulty understanding how to use the traffic circles. Although they had been in place for almost four decades, many collisions were still happening. To help reduce the number of crashes, the transportation department replaced five circles with intersections in the 1980s and 90s.

Still liking the traffic circle idea, the city started constructing more in the early 2000s. They have just been building the new ones in less busy areas, such as residential neighbourhoods.

Transit Hotel

Fort Road and 66 Street

It opened on September 11, 1908, in the part of Edmonton known as Packingtown for all the meat packing facilities in the area. Patrick Dwyer financed many projects in north Edmonton, including the Transit, which cost $50,000 to build. It had a tavern and forty rooms that cost $1.50 a night. The hotel was one of the few commercial buildings with modern amenities, such as hot and cold running water, lavatories, telephones and electricity. Dwyer moved to British Columbia and wanted to sell the Transit. In 1924, the hotel sold for just over $10,000. This place made it for ninety-three years before closing its doors in 2017.

It reopened on September 20, 2021, with the Transit Smokehouse & BBQ on the main level, as significant work happened to preserve this place, including the original bar.

Trolley Buses

The trolley bus system, a significant part of Edmonton's transportation history, started in September 1939. At its peak, a fleet of one hundred and thirty-seven trolley buses had a route length of one hundred and twenty-seven kilometres, operating from 101 Street and Jasper Avenue to 95 Street and 111 Avenue. By the end of October of that year, service had started on another route to the south, running to 99 Street and 82 Avenue over the Low Level Bridge.

Trolleys were the staple of the transit systems for most of the twentieth century.

In 2008, the city was still home to forty-nine of the one hundred trolley buses ordered in 1981. These buses were unique, being the only trolley buses ever built with the General Motors' New Look' body style. This design was mostly seen on the over 44,000 motor buses. Five trolley buses are still around in various bus museums. One of those buses is in the Reynolds Alberta Museum in Wetaskiwin.

On June 18, 2008, the city council voted seven to six in favour of phasing out the trolley bus system by 2010. However, the council decided to discontinue the trolley bus service sooner to save money, citing the high maintenance costs and the need for more modern and efficient transit options. The last day of service was May 2, 2009.

Union Bank Building

Jasper Avenue and 100 Street

It was constructed in 1910 during Edmonton's economic boom. Although more than ten banks were on Jasper Avenue between 100 and 101 Streets, this remains the only one pre-World War I. The bank entrance also served upstairs offices and third-floor living quarters for bank employees.

In 1928, Winnipeg's James Richardson and Sons Limited bought this building. It served as an Edmonton base for their grain trading and stock broking business. Then, in 1969, the North-West Trust Company occupied it until 1982, when it became a bank again.

Following many years of neglect, the building was restored and re-opened as the Union Bank Inn.

They received their municipal historic designation on August 20, 1996.

University of Alberta's Heating and Cooling Plants

84 Avenue at 115 Street

The heating plant was built in 1959 to supply electricity to the Greater Campus Area by producing their own power. Producing heat in a central plant is about twenty-five percent more efficient than using stand-alone boilers in the buildings. Additional steam turbine generators were added in 1994 and 2000.

Also on Campus is a Cooling Plant that uses cold river water as a source and a Thermal Energy Storage Unit that can produce up to 5,000 tons of chilled water.

Connecting everything is a ten-kilometre underground service corridor that runs from the plants to the buildings on Campus.

Four control centres, one in the heating plant, one in each cooling plant and one in the electrical shop, can operate everything.

The heating plant can produce six hundred and fifty tonnes of steam per hour! These two towers produce steam, partly responsible for fogging the downtown area during winter when wind/inversion conditions occur.

Valley Zoo

Buena Vista Road

A search began to find a replacement for the previous Edmonton Zoo at Borden Park. It was built in 1931 and torn down to expand Northlands Park. The city invited a representative from another well-respected zoo to help advise on a new location. Areas that received consideration included Whitemud Park and Mill Creek. When this location opened on July 1, 1959, it was initially called the Storyland Valley Zoo, a fairy-tale theme over five acres. The construction cost was $500,000. Admission was ten cents for kids and twenty-five cents for adults.

After fifty years, the Edmonton Valley Zoo was showing signs of age. In 2014, the conclusion of a fifty-million-dollar revitalization project breathed new life into this beloved institution. The transformation was complete, and the zoo had grown to an impressive seventy acres, a commitment to wildlife conservation. It was now home to over three hundred and fifty animals, a significant increase from its humble beginnings. And at the heart of this growth was one of its oldest residents, Lucy the Elephant. She came to the zoo on May 19, 1977, after being orphaned in Sri Lanka.

Valleyview Manor

Jasper Avenue and 122 Street

Built in 1961 for about one million dollars, this was one of the first high-rise apartment buildings in the city. It has forty-five units, over 65,000 square feet. The building was constructed to attract people to live downtown, in a high-density neighbourhood and try to slow down suburban sprawl, which sounds familiar to today's world. It was advertised as Edmonton's 'New Home of Gracious Living,' with proximity to the downtown core. The building boasts many high-end qualities, including a great view overlooking the river valley, luxurious marble finishes, and the convenience of underground parking.

This structure added to the city's skyline and helped build up the west end of downtown. One of the most predominant residents was Francis Winspear, an accountant, businessman, and philanthropist, after whom the Winspear Centre is named.

Valleyview Manor received its municipal historic designation in November 2010.

Velodrome

88 Street and 68 Avenue

The city constructed the facility in 1977 for competitive cycling during the 1978 Commonwealth Games. The facility came alive for cycling competitions at the 1983 Summer Universiade Games. The Argyll Velodrome was closed between 1989 and 1996. Later, it hosted the 2001 National Track Cycling Championships and the 2005 World Masters' Games.

The track has been privately operated since 1996. A new indoor track in Coronation Park is due to open in 2026. The facility would be only the second indoor triathlon training centre globally.

Victoria Park

River Valley Road

This park was named after Queen Victoria, born on May 24, 1819. She was crowned when she was just 18 years old, and her reign lasted sixty-three years. Victoria Day holiday is also named after her. The observance of Queen Victoria's birthday, also known as the 'Mother of Confederation,' dates back to 1845 in Canada. But it wasn't until she died in 1901 that "Victoria Day" became a national holiday. In 1921, it was renamed "Empire Day." The aim was to create an attitude that would produce patriotic citizens for the British Empire.

Initially, this area was known as Hudson's Bay Company Flats before the city bought this parkland. In 1912, the name changed due to a petition at City Hall to identify the park with a famous woman. This area has many amenities, including a 4km walking trail, a cricket pitch, picnic sites, a restaurant, a Pavilion in the winter, a skating oval and Park IceWay path. The golf course is Canada's oldest city-run golf facility, dating back to 1896.

The completion of the name change didn't happen until 1957 when the Edmonton Municipal Golf Course became the Victoria Golf Course. Legislation passed in 1952 declaring the first Monday preceding May 24 as the Victoria Day celebration. Not all provinces recognize Victoria Day as a statutory holiday. Some don't even recognize it at all! In 1980, there was a movement to bring back Empire Day, as that was the year the Star Wars movie The Empire Strikes Back was released.

Victoria School

101 Street and 108 Avenue

When this school opened in 1911, it was called Edmonton High School. Two years later, the name was changed to Victoria. The original building cost $150,000 as additions happened many times, including 1948, 49, 50, 56, 62, and 63. The original building was demolished in 1963.

Victoria had many firsts, including the first school built in the city for high school students, the first to have a swimming pool, and the first to have a cafeteria. In 1938, seven hundred and twenty-six students were enrolled here, now over eighteen hundred and fifty from kindergarten to grade twelve. A few well-known alumni who attended this school were TV and movie actor Leslie Neilson from the Naked Gun movies, World War I flying aces Wop May, and Roy Brown, who is recognized and credited with shooting down the Red Baron.

Virginia Park School

109 Avenue and 73 Street

This place opened in 1948 for $81,000. The school was named after the former Virginia Park Greenhouse that was nearby in 1912. The school operated well for three decades until it almost closed in 1976 because of low enrollment. The principal at the time had a master's degree in arts and had the idea to transform the school, emphasizing the fine arts. That was a new concept for Edmonton, so the school board agreed to the program and arranged for $10,000 in spending to start it. The program is still the core value for this elementary school as they now have an enrollment of one hundred-plus students.

W.E. Ross Building

82 Avenue and 103 Street

Built in 1894 for $40,000, the Ross Block is not just a building but a cornerstone of Edmonton's history. It is the second oldest building in the city, with Strathcona Hotel being the first, its neighbour across the road, constructed three years earlier. The Ross Block was one of the first brick buildings on Whyte Avenue, and it housed Strathcona's first hardware, plumbing, and tinsmith business. Over the years, it has been a feed store, a restaurant, a clothing store, and a nightclub on the ground floor, and Strathcona's first meeting hall and cultural centre, a Masonic Lodge, before being converted into apartments. If these walls could talk, they would share stories that have shaped our community over the past century.

In 1976, the W.E. Ross Building was officially recognized for its historical significance, a testament to its enduring legacy.

Wellington Bridge

102 Avenue by 131 Street

The Ramsay Ravine and the Groat Ravine obstructed a direct east-to-west road to connect Edmonton with the Town of West Jasper Place. Wellington Bridge was constructed in 1932 to make the commute quicker.

Motorists drive over this bridge daily and might not even notice it due to the trees growing around it. This bridge is nearing the end of its service life. A new impressive cement arch bridge will replace the current one with another. It will increase the width to include vehicles and a shared-use path for pedestrians and bikes. Bridge demolition will happen after the west LRT line completion north of here. This project will begin sometime in 2025.

West Edmonton Mall

170 Street and 87 Avenue

Phase One of the mall opened on September 15, 1981. The anchor tenants were Eatons, Sears, The Bay, and Safeway. These stores, along with two hundred and twenty other retail stores and services, formed the backbone of the mall's early retail offerings. The grand opening celebrations included a ribbon-cutting ceremony, speeches, fireworks, and many prizes, including thousands of dollars of gift certificates and a trip to Fiji.

Phase Two opened in 1983, almost doubling the mall to four hundred and sixty stores and services. The highlight of this phase was the opening of the Galaxyland Amusement Park, the world's largest indoor amusement park. This park featured a variety of thrilling rides, including the Mindbender, the world's largest indoor triple loop roller coaster, and the Space Shot, a vertical drop tower. Placed in a pillar by the entrance of Galaxyland is a time capsule that will be opened in 2033. Also in this phase was an

NHL-sized skating rink, which the Edmonton Oilers would use as a second practice facility.

Phase Three, in 1985, added the unique themed shopping areas of Europa Boulevard and Bourbon Street, replicating streets from Europe and New Orleans. Also included was the World Waterpark with slides and the world's largest indoor wave pool. Also included was the Deep Sea Adventure with live dolphins, the world's largest indoor miniature golf course, and the world's largest indoor lake. Four full-size submarines and a full-size replica of the historic ship, the Santa Maria, completed phase three. The Fantasyland Hotel was added in 1986, with three hundred and fifty-four rooms, including one hundred and twenty themed fantasy rooms, making it a truly unique destination.

Phase Four, in 1998, an IMAX theatre was added, and the first Simons Store opened outside of Quebec in the mall in 2012.

West Edmonton Mall, a historical marvel, was once promoted as the 'Eighth Wonder of the World.' The mall, covering the equivalent of one hundred and four football fields, held the Guinness Book of World Records as the world's largest shopping centre for twenty-four years.

West Jasper Place Neighbourhood

Meadowlark Road and 156 Street

In the early 1900s, West Jasper Place was home to a few hundred families farming the community. By the 1930s, this area was experiencing significant population growth. When Edmonton increased taxes, many families moved out of the city and settled in West Jasper Place. Edmonton also imposed an early closing time for stores of 6:00 P.M., where Jasper Place stores were open until 9:00 P.M.

In 1947, the area's population boomed again with the discovery of oil, making West Jasper Place the largest hamlet in Alberta. In early 1950, it became a village, doubling the population to 8,900 in just two years. Later that year, it became a town. Jasper Place was called 'Mud City' due to its lack of paved streets. In August 1964, West Jasper Place, with a population of over 37,000, was Canada's largest town before amalgamating with Edmonton.

West Jasper Place is also known for having the first Edmonton area drive-in theatre. It opened on the southeast corner of 87 Avenue and 156 Street in 1949 for $160,000. It had the largest screen in the country, measuring forty-seven feet high by fifty-five feet wide and room for six hundred and fifty vehicles. It closed in 1971.

Westglen School

127 Street and 109 Avenue

This school's original name was Mountglen, which opened in 1940. It took less than five months to construct, as the building permit was issued on July 6 and the official opening on November 30. That's unheard of by today's standards, and it only costs $155,000 to build. The school was heated by coal and was only one of two schools in Edmonton that opened during the Second World War, the other being Glenora, which opened two weeks prior. This place started as a high school until 1957, then operated as elementary and junior high until 1971. Since then, it has been a kindergarten to grade six school with an enrollment of about three hundred and fifty students.

Westminster Apartments

100 Avenue and 114 Street

This three-story, twenty-four-suite complex was built in 1912 for $65,000. The Westminster was ahead of its time and was a testament to modernity with all the amenities, including telephones, in every apartment. It was considered very elegant for a pre-First World War construction, standing tall among other multi-family buildings in the area, such as the LeMarchand Mansion.

The location was not just desirable but was a bustling residential area. It attracted white-collar workers and prominent Edmontonians, including the first Lieutenant Governor of Alberta, George Bulyea. This place, a cornerstone of Edmonton's past, received its municipal historic designation in 1996.

Westmount School

111 Avenue and 130 Street

Construction began in 1913, but two months later, work stopped due to financial difficulties from the School Board and a shortage of building supplies. Construction continued on and off for seven years. Part of the school opened in April 1915, and the second floor was finally completed in 1920. The final cost was $200,000, and this became Edmonton Public's first junior high school. A high school section was opened in 1927, and nine years later, it became an elementary, junior, and senior high school. Since 1970, this place has been home to students from grades seven to nine.

Westwood Transit Garage

118 Avenue and 106A Street

The garage opened in 1961 and operated until the last ETS bus left on February 8, 2020, a day before the new Kathleen Andrews facility opened on Fort Road by the Yellowhead Trail.

Edmonton Transit Service began operations in October 1908 with a fleet of four streetcars, which it operated until 1951. Since then, the city bus fleet has consisted of trolley, gas, diesel, and electric buses.

After fifty-nine years of dispatching buses, the old Transit Garage, a symbol of our city's transit history, has gracefully completed its service. It was demolished, and the land was sold to NAIT.

Whitemud Park & Equine Centre

Fox Drive and Keillor Road

Fred Keillor moved to Edmonton in 1912 to start a medical practice. He served in the Royal Army Medical Corps in the First World War before returning to Edmonton. In 1918, he purchased this large piece of property from the Imperial Bank after the great flood of 1915.

Keillor believed in the benefits of outdoor recreation, so he opened an area to the public for horseback riding, cross-country skiing, hiking and canoeing. Keillor built a beautiful stone house on the property, and he lived here until 1925 before moving to the Garneau neighbourhood, but he still owned the farmland. He donated a portion of his property to the city for a road to provide better access to his farm and Whitemud Park.

Besides farming, Keillor was the city's coroner and served two terms as a City Alderman. He refused his pay cheque for the job and had a road named after him. It was a great shortcut to the university area before it was closed to vehicle traffic in 1995. The road collapsed a few years later due to an unstable river bank. Fred Keillor also donated 500 spruce trees from his farm to be planted throughout Edmonton.

Yardbird Suite

Gateway Boulevard and Tommy Banks Way

The original Yardbird Suite opened its doors on Whyte Avenue in 1957. It was created to promote jazz music in the city. The company moved several times, including 1962, 1967, and 1973, before settling at this location in 1984.

The Yardbird Suite is unique in Canada. It is the longest-running jazz club and the only facility in the country that operates entirely by volunteers, showcasing the power of community and shared passion. You can become a member to help promote its mission to advance jazz music through performance and education. And to build on its long history as a world-renowned community venue for jazz performance and education open to all.

They average seventy-five concerts every season, from September to June, on the weekends.

YEG
Edmonton International Airport
Airport Road and Queen Elizabeth II Highway

It opened for passenger service on November 15, 1960. The Spar Aviation hangar was used as a temporary terminal, which lasted until 1963 when the new terminal opened. It cost ten million dollars and was ready a year ahead of schedule.

The airport's passenger numbers grew from 394,000 in 1962 to over eight million in 2018. YEG has undergone significant construction programs, such as the new south terminal, the Central Hall for security screening, a new cargo apron, additional gates, and expanded parking. A new departure ramp and access road to the south are complete.

YEG is Canada's largest airport by land area. More than half the land is still available to accommodate growth, as the Edmonton Metro Region predicts to have about 2.2 million people by 2044, and the airport will keep growing with the population.

Special Acknowledgments

With any project, there are always people who help you achieve the end result. I want to thank my wife Tammy for her patience while I researched these stories and for her assistance in proofreading my grammar.

Bob Layton who encouraged me to put this book together and shared his knowledge on publishing books.

Thank you to the viewers of Global Edmonton Television. Your interest in my stories is the reason I created this book.

Follow me on:

Shane Blakely - In & Above Edmonton

aerial_edmonton

Manufactured by Amazon.ca
Acheson, AB

32413582R00146